Photos and Phantasms

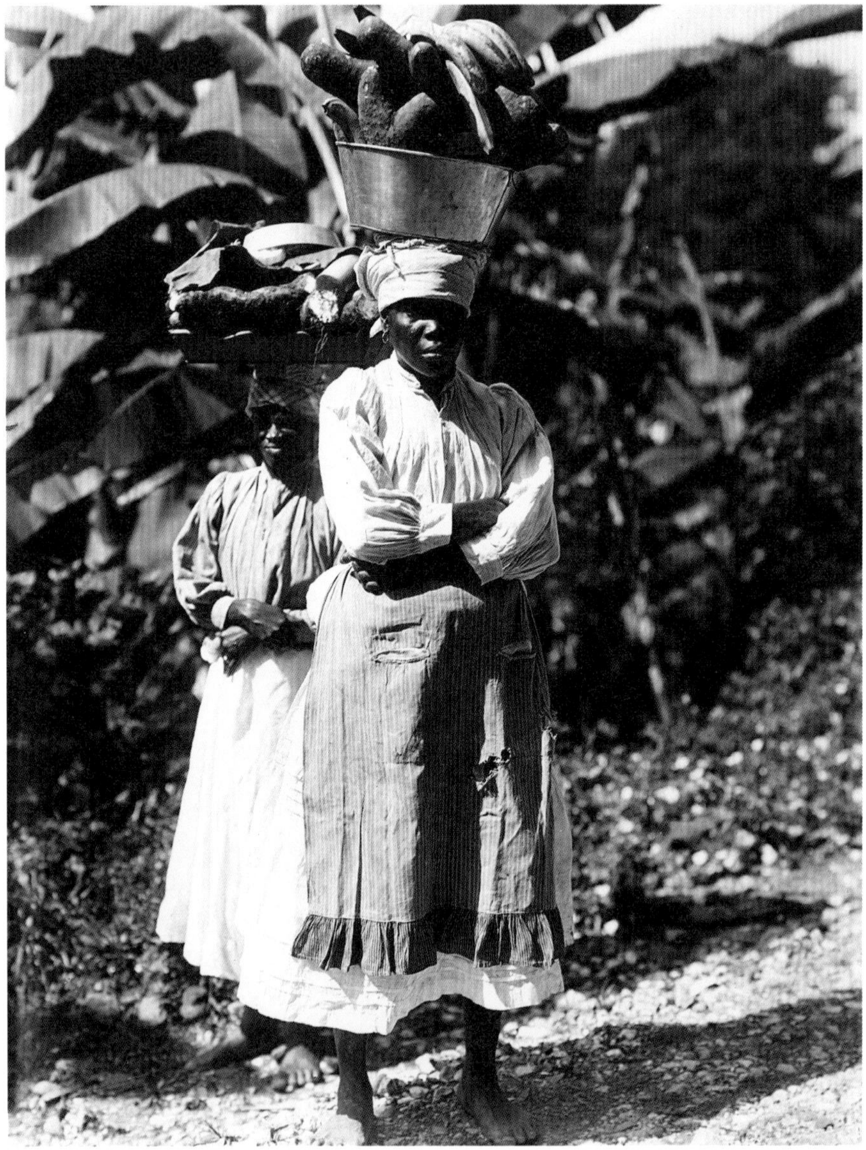

Photos and Phantasms

HARRY JOHNSTON'S PHOTOGRAPHS OF THE CARIBBEAN

The British Council
Royal Geographical Society
[WITH THE INSTITUTE OF BRITISH GEOGRAPHERS]
London · 1998

Published by The British Council
10 Spring Gardens, London SW1A 2BN

ISBN 0 86355 384 2

Exhibition organised by Brett Rogers and Sean Williams, Visual Arts, The British Council, London

Designed and typeset in Hoefler Text by Dalrymple
Printed in England by BAS Printers Ltd

Front cover: A Jamaican Negro, *cat.35*
Back cover: A Haitian Market, Haiti, *cat.15*
Frontispiece: Negro Peasant Woman, Jamaica, *cat.47*

EXHIBITION TOUR

National Gallery of Jamaica, Kingston, Jamaica
29 March – 2 May 1998

National Museum of Trinidad and Tobago
Port of Spain, Trinidad
12 – 30 May 1998

Queen's Park Gallery, Bridgetown, Barbados
7 – 30 June 1998

Fototeca de Cuba, Havana, Cuba
12 July – 6 August 1998

Le Musée d'Art Haitien, Port au Prince, Haiti
16 September – 17 October 1998

Preface

Renegotiation and reassessment have been at the heart of both the current exhibition project and the original enterprise in which Johnston himself was involved. Johnston's remarkable photographs began life as illustrations for an ethnographic study which he considered would contribute to a re-evaluation of Caribbean culture in America and Europe. One of our main intentions in mounting this joint Royal Geographical Society / British Council exhibition specifically for the Caribbean has been to generate debate about the nature of Johnston's imagery and allow local audiences to assess for themselves the contribution, value and legacy of Johnston's formidable output. As so few photographic archives exist in the region, the return of this material would appear to be an apt way of completing the cycle begun by Johnston himself some ninety years ago. This project forms part of a broader policy, initiated by Visual Arts a decade ago, of repatriating facsimile photographs to their country of origin. So far, exhibitions of material drawn from various British archives have been mounted for Turkey, Cyprus, India, China, Madagascar and Papua New Guinea. It also marks the first occasion on which the Council has toured a photographic exhibition outside the English-speaking islands of the Caribbean.

In realising this project over the course of the past two years, we have been very much guided by our curator, Dr Petrine Archer-Straw. We extend our thanks to her for undertaking the original research on Johnston's life as well as the subsequent selection of work for this exhibition. Dr Archer-Straw's personal engagement with the material, combined with her vivid articulation of current issues within Caribbean scholarship, has resulted in a stimulating catalogue essay which addresses contemporary assumptions about colonial photography as well as the social and political history of the region. Whilst not overlooking the complex nature of photographic representation nor the questionable theories underlying Johnston's own enterprise, Dr Archer-Straw successfully argues that his work deserves to be looked at afresh. Johnston's imagery may be best understood as a palimpsest, in which new layers of meaning have been superimposed over older ones, or rearticulated, every time they are placed in a different context.

This is the first of what, we hope, will become a series of collaborations with the Society, whose photographic archives remain a vastly undervalued resource both within the UK and abroad. We warmly thank Dr Rita Gardner and Joanna Scadden of the Royal Geographical Society with the Institute of British Geographers for their invaluable advice and support with the current project, as well as Sean Williams of Visual Arts, The British Council, who has skilfully coordinated all aspects of this project.

BRETT ROGERS
Deputy Director, Visual Arts, The British Council

Foreword

The Royal Geographical Society was founded in 1830 and from that date has maintained a Library and a Map Room to, as the Royal Charter states, 'contribute to the progress of geographical knowledge'. The holdings reflect the development of the study of geography throughout the world from the mediaeval period to the present day, providing especially in the last 167 years, an unrivalled insight into the activities and publications of geographers, travellers and environmental scientists. It is a unique attribute of the collection that much of the material has been donated and that many of the donors have been the actual originators, be they authors, surveyors, artists, cartographers, or their families. To these may be added photographers, since, once the camera became more – or – less portable in the 1860s, it was rapidly adopted as a significant method of recording geography in the field alongside the diary and survey observations.

Since the 1860s, the Society's photographic archive has grown steadily, currently amounting to some half a million images. These provide the modern viewer with a record, not only of the changes in the technology available to the photographer, but also of the changes in the political and social milieu in which the photographer operated, both at home and in the field. Such changes continue to the present day. The vision of contemporary photographers is as much a product of the late twentieth century as Harry Johnston's photographs are an indication of his Victorian influences and upbringing.

The Society's Picture Archive is a particularly good vantage point from which to widen our mental and visual horizons by examining the changing values and realities recorded by people whose outlook, values and circumstances may be quite different from our own. In this context, the Society is delighted to be given this opportunity to display a small, but very significant element of its holdings in this exhibition *Photos and Phantasms*.

The possibility of disseminating these images has come about only recently through the conservation work on negatives in the Picture Archive, which brought to light the original glass plate negatives taken by Harry Johnston during his working life. The Johnston negatives number over a thousand, and show scenes from Africa and America, as well as the Caribbean. They have remained unseen since they were presented to the Society in 1933 by the Johnston family. This exhibition shows for the first time the extent of Harry Johnston's vision and employs photographic prints which have been handsomely crafted from the original glass plate negatives by Mike Gray, using nineteenth century photographic procedures. Both the Society and the British Council are indebted to Mike Gray for his contribution to this project.

That these photographs can be seen at all is

the culmination of much hard work and fruitful collaboration by the hosting institutions and especially by the British Council. The Society is most grateful to all who have made this creative dialogue between the UK and the Caribbean possible, not least in matters of geographical and environmental interest. This happy circumstance owes much to the labours of Dr Archer-Straw whose intensive research has given much needed background information to Harry Johnston's photographs. The Society is most appreciative of her contribution.

It is perhaps fitting that through the rediscovery of Johnston's work, those who see this exhibition, as well as those who have brought it into being, will themselves be able to develop some new understanding of the thoughts and feelings that both shape our past and present, and through this, to find opportunities of working together for the future of ourselves and our environment.

JOANNA SCADDEN
Picture Library Manager

DR ANDREW TATHAM
Keeper, Royal Geographical Society with IBG

ACKNOWLEDGEMENTS

For their generous support and assistance with this project Dr Petrine Archer-Straw would like to thank: Gerald Alexis, Musée d'Art Haitien, Haiti; Dr David Boxer, Jamaica; Mary Beckles, Barbados; Georges Corvington, Haiti; Dr Michael Dash, Jamaica; Mario Diaz, Fototeca de Cuba, Havana; Patricia Dunn, West Indies Collection, University of the West Indies, Jamaica; Vel Lewis, National Museum of Trinidad and Tobago; Margaret Guercy, Vice Consul, Haiti; Knolly Moses, Panmedia, Jamaica; Professor Rex Nettleford, Jamaica; Joanna Norcup, London; Jose Noceda, Centro Wilfredo Lam, Havana; Veerle Poupaye-Rammelaere, Jamaica; Samuel Parris, Jamaican High Commission, London; Harclyde Walcott, Studio Art, Jamaica; Andrea Wells, National Cultural Foundation, Barbados.

Photos and Phantasms: Harry Johnston's Photographs of the Caribbean

Petrine Archer-Straw

The recovery of a cultural heritage with a literary and historical tradition not entirely derived from colonial roots is a powerful symbol of the Caribbean's independence. The region's scholars are revisiting sites of 'discovery', slavery and emancipation and finding a history that better represents those who live here now. The region's countries are creating national heroes, myths and legends that challenge and counter colonial perspectives and inspire the creation of a collective consciousness with a sense of unity, nationhood and history.[1]

Despite the deconstruction of that inherited literature, our visual perception of the past remains vague. Till now, that perception has been reliant on literary stereotypes, where the 'native' is either a savage or merry, mischievous child.[2] In these histories black societies are more often described negatively in opposition to white civilisation as barbaric and chaotic. Such stereotypes are held in the minds-eye, and loom in the imagination, filling the gaps that our visual ignorance of the past creates.[3]

The photographs of Sir Harry Johnston[4] in this exhibition may help recover a visual heritage that discards those stereotypes. Johnston's archive provides evidence to show how the Caribbean's post-emancipation peasantry lived. A compelling feature of Johnston's photography is the way he captures everyday life in the Caribbean at the turn of the century.[5] His scenes, of markets, farmers and workers in rural settings depict a vivid and accurate record of a lifestyle that has changed considerably in this century. Johnston researched that lifestyle thoroughly, along with the Caribbean's history, environment and society for his book *The Negro in the New World,* where many of these photographs were first seen.

Not everyone will view these images comfortably. Johnston's photography confronts us with a view of the past that may be too intimately revealing. These photographs defy post-independence political ideas that present the region as polyglot, multi-cultural and hybrid. Instead, we find a Caribbean community that is predominantly black. The images also indicate more clearly than can be discerned today, that the peasantry was tied to an African heritage and the land. Till now, the absence of this type of imagery allowed those in the Caribbean to cultivate a 'self-hate' that created new personas or what could be called a 'colonial self' that is 'coloured' rather than 'black'.

Others may object to colonial photography taken in support of Johnston's questionable theories about race in the Caribbean. Johnston combined his avid reading of colonial history and Darwinist evolutionary theories to document what he called 'the inferior races of the world.' He established clear hierarchies based on racial characteristics, using the white European male as the standard. To disown these images in *Photos and Phantasms* because of this context is, however, to lose sight of their value. To judge the subjects of these photographs as innocent or complicit, or to paint Johnston as a typical 'colonial', short-changes a larger discussion about how whites and blacks negotiated each other's identities during this era. Discomfort is an inevitable consequence of really 'seeing' these images and the complex investigation they provoke.

This essay exposes biases, past and present, to make the subtleties that informed Johnston's photography more visible. It also questions our need today to refashion the past and retell history by constructing our own vision for the 'New World', as Johnston called it.[6] A creolised history recognises the interrelatedness of ideas whether originating in Europe or Africa. Within the Caribbean, our understanding of ourselves is seen in the way the two dominant cultures of Europe and Africa interacted and accommodated each other. As the image on this catalogue's back cover illustrates, even as blacks assert themselves in the camera's frame, Johnston's shadowy presence intrudes unwittingly. This essay is about what is revealed on both sides of the camera's lens.[7]

The voyeurism in this photograph has another side. Anonymity is inherent in this type of colonial photography. Including Johnston's biographical detail in this essay helps the viewer to understand how the colonial vision was shaped and opens up more general discussions about the colonial mentality.

The Jamaican writer H.G. DeLisser referred to the Englishman as a 'negrophilist', a lover of black people. It is hard to reconcile Johnston's racial theories with such a term. At the turn of the century, Johnston's interest in people from Africa and its Diaspora would have been progressive, liberal and peculiar for the period. After abolition, few championed the black cause, albeit in such a patronising manner. *Negro in the New World* gives a detailed account of the white man's atrocities against blacks between 1770 and 1840 and is critical of the treatment of blacks. Johnston later noted that because of its 'plain speaking' the book was 'unpopular in England, and almost tabued [sic] in the United States, though its writer sought to tell nothing but the truth'.[8]

Today, we might presume that Johnston's work was unpopular because of its racism. More likely, it was unpopular because of its pro-black sentiments and its judgment on colonial history. Discussing British historical writers of the period, Caribbean historian Eric Williams says that most were unrepentant imperialists who believed that West Indians were on racial grounds unfit for self-government. Johnston, on the other hand, believed that they had experienced an accelerated development and proved themselves capable of governing their own affairs.[9] The images in *Photos and Phantasms* are intended to support Johnston's theories about New World blacks. They demonstrate a self-reliance that would prove prophetic as their nations moved towards self government and independence.

AN ENGLISH MAN IN THE NEW WORLD

The photographs in this exhibition were taken between 1908–09, when Harry Johnston travelled through the Caribbean with his companion Arthur Greaves.[10] They took over 250 photographs on the last leg of a longer journey through the Americas.

The trip grew out of Johnston's friendship with the United States President Theodore Roosevelt. Both shared interests in imperial expansion, the new sciences of geography and anthropology, and Africa. Roosevelt invited Johnston to America to discuss Roosevelt's forthcoming expedition in Africa.[11] Roosevelt was also keen to learn more about negroes in the Caribbean and asked Johnston for information about the political stability of Cuba, Haiti, Jamaica and Panama.[12]

Johnston arrived in the Caribbean on the eve of America's departure from Cuba and in the wake of its military occupation of Haiti.[13] Fresh from talks with Roosevelt about the plight of North American blacks and hints about the possibility of a 'Liberia type' home[14] in the Caribbean, Johnston conceived a working trip to further his comparative studies of blacks in Africa and extend it to the New World. While in America he had consulted with black scholars such as W.E. du Bois and Booker T. Washington about the conditions African Americans were experiencing there.[15] Johnston began his investigations in the Caribbean by looking at the conditions of negroes under Spanish, British and French rule. As an anthropologist, Johnston was eager to prove his theory that the Caribbean negro was more highly developed than the African negro because of colonialism,[16] and that there were even more subtle distinctions between negroes of the Caribbean resulting from different forms of colonisation. Johnston's botanical and environmental interests also fuelled these concerns: climate, natural resources, diseases, agriculture and island infrastructure affected his assessment, each island presenting a different ecosystem.

Johnston's writing shows that he firmly believed that a rational methodology could be applied to his project. His search for negro types in the Caribbean was systematic, and consistent with his need to make comparisons. Earlier photographs taken in Africa vividly demonstrate his approach to the task. Johnston shows naked blacks positioned beside measuring instruments or posed front side and back before the camera, almost as if he were examining another species.[17] Fortunately, such imagery is not a feature of his work in the Caribbean. But this earlier methodology is evident in his consistent positioning and framing of negro men and women in rural settings (cat.47, 37 and 53) and the disconcerting image in Haiti of a black man and an agave (cat.28).

Johnston did not have a traditional public school education, so he was unschooled in the classics. Education was not urgent for him because his family was reasonably well off. His liberal arts education at Stockwell Grammar was an early sign of his modernity. At seventeen, he studied languages as an evening student at King's College, and art at South London Art College. A year later he was admitted to the Royal Academy of Arts. His interest in zoological specimens gave him a lucrative part-time income, illustrating books for the new sciences of biology, geography, anthropology. The combination of art, languages and a developing interest in the sciences marked Johnston as a new breed of scholar whose skills met colonialism's need for exploration, expansion and documentation.[18]

Johnston's first expedition was to Portuguese Angola where he recorded the flora and fauna en route and documented species peculiar to the region.[19] More significant missions followed, including the Kilimanjaro Expedition in 1886.

Even more important than his linguistic and scientific abilities were his diplomatic skills, which the British used frequently. It suited them to send Johnston on these expeditions, ostensibly as a geographer / naturalist. But as he became more familiar with Africa's peoples and their power structure, he was given greater freedom to negotiate on the colonial power's behalf.[20] Johnston thrived on the responsibility, and was zealous to learn more about these newly acquired territories.[21] By the 1880's, Johnston had become a career diplomat specialising in Africa. He was appointed Vice Consul for the Cameroons and Niger Delta in 1885 and by 1893, Commissioner of Nyasaland, the new British protectorate, later called Rhodesia.

Johnston developed a reputation as a trouble shooter, renowned for his affability in diplomacy. Europe's presence in Africa had shifted in half a century from the wide-eyed explorations of missionaries such as David Livingstone to more calculated conquests. The scramble for Africa was underway and 'new men' like Harry Johnston were the major players in European rivalry. Johnston had a good working knowledge of African territories and negotiated a number of treaties on behalf of the Colonial Office.

Even with the pressures of travel and diplomatic work, Johnston was able to continue his visual documentation of Africa and interest in photography. His use of the camera was prolific and, although used initially for the practical purpose of recording the rare or difficult to render, Johnston already demonstrated an artistic sensitivity to subjects. His interest in detailed work, difficult angles and unusual juxtapositions, undermined his own theories of objectivity, demonstrating a combination of realism and romanticism that is never entirely documentary or ever frivolous. This tension between two photographic forms adds rather than detracts from the image represented. Simple images are ennobled and / or shrouded in nostalgia as Johnston tries to preserve his visions of the region. Because of his early fine art training, there is an ever present contradiction between art and science in his approach, which softens the inherent racism of some images, or alternatively lends a botanical eye to his floral photography.

Photography in Johnston's time was still an experimental practice of cumbersome equipment, light sensitive instruments and a cocktail of chemicals and metals. Along with the skill to manage these tools, good photography required a discerning eye and artistic sensitivity. Johnston mastered all these variables. His photographs are well composed within the frame. They are bold and incisive. Light is controlled rather than accepted, sometimes subtly to suggest mood and nuances, at other times dramatically, to define and enrich images. Johnston also favoured stereographs, a photographic form that when viewed through a stereoscope seemed three dimensional. Even without these tricks of the eye Johnston's images have a depth and resolution that enhance their realism.

Johnston took hundreds of photographs, presumably to accompany his numerous Royal Geographical Society lectures. As a geographer, Johnston wanted to give an accurate picture of the countries he visited and his archive is a visual travelogue. Johnston's photography also demonstrates his environmental concerns. He wanted to capture aspects of Caribbean wildlife and nature that he believed to be threatened with extinction or by the negative effects of urbanisation. Rape of the mountains for fuel burning woods, indiscriminate shooting of endangered animals and birds, and what he saw as the lack of sensitivity and knowledge that Caribbeans had for their own environment are discussed in *Negro in the New World* and other texts.[22]

Johnston journeyed around the islands by boat, and through each island by road and railway. He travelled routes that were becoming increasingly popular because of developing tourism and an agricultural economy in the Caribbean. Although the time Johnston spent in each island varied, what he sought from each appears to have been the same; to flesh out his understanding of the negro. As a naturalist, Johnston examined the relationship of Diaspora negroes to their new environment. He believed that the Afro-Caribbean was adapting quickly and becoming better suited to the terrain and climate than other races. Images such as *Cactus House* (cat.3) evoke this kinship between the Afro-Caribbean and the land. Johnston was particularly interested in how negroes in the Caribbean withstood diseases. He saw health management, drainage and mosquito control, as markers of civilisation. Disease, inadequate water facilities, poor drainage, and unsanitary conditions were signs that the islands could still lapse into chaos and barbarism. Johnston measured their economic development to see if ex-slaves could function in modern industry. He studied their attitudes to work to determine whether they could be integrated into the increasingly mechanised production of bananas, cane, tobacco and coffee.

BLACKS IN A BRAVE NEW WORLD

At the turn of the century, photography in the Caribbean was still the preserve of the wealthy, who were hardly excited by images of the rural peasantry. Images taken by family business photographers such as the Duperleys in Jamaica,[23] and the Valdezes of Cuba[24] show a colonially cultured and upwardly mobile bourgeoisie anxious to keep formal memories of themselves, a narrative far different from Johnston's. In Jamaica, Duperley's hatted, suited colonial subjects inhabit artificial studio settings, perhaps the verandah of a lavishly plant strewn colonial mansion, or with the prop of an automobile.[25]

Johnston's photographs display none of this artifice. They document the peasantry outdoor, using techniques that were arduous and totally public.[26] Along with portraiture, we see dramatic landscapes, bustling market scenes, sparsely populated country roads. The photographer's interests allow us to view their lifestyle in period detail. The images in *Photos and Phantasms* capture a mood that defies both the colonial and contemporary historians' reading of the period and people.[27] They are bold, assertive images that speak about post-emancipation settlement, industry, camaraderie, resistance and independence. The images present an alternative to the social historians' view that this era was one of planter disillusionment and peasant resentments. They show people coping, hustling and challenging the system to secure their own economic viability.

The last half of the nineteenth century saw the dismantling of the slavery 'machine'[28] and the transition of Caribbean people from the institution of slavery to free status. Although emancipation came sporadically through the region, most islanders had shed slavery and plantations for small farming and subsistence holdings by the turn of the century. Historians still argue whether post-emancipation apprenticeship schemes were a significant economic shift from slavery.[29] Despite the ex-slaves desire to have greater control over their free time and labour, there were restrictions on mobility, tenancy and use of plantation property. Their small wages also limited their options. What is clear is that the plantation system remained at the hub of economic life.[30] Although the psychological advantages of freedom were significant, the economic benefits for the peasantry were negligible in the turgid economies of these small islands.

Johnston's pictures of Maroon Town in the hills of Portland, Jamaica, echo a narrative of resistance and independence. This community of slave descendants, initially called the Cimarrones (mountaineers), negotiated autonomy and separate governance of their ex-slave settlements in 1740.[31] It is significant that all views of this village are taken from the outside looking in; the photographer is forced to be the voyeur, and his image of the maroons is controlled by what they allow him to see. *In Maroon Country* (cat.53), a lone figure washing in the river shields himself (?) from the intrusive nature of the camera. Covering his head with a sheet is a passive, or, at least, evasive response. But the European outsider, used to a more conciliatory approach from blacks, interprets this as hostile.[32] By contrast, *Haitian Woman with Children* (cat.25) is openly challenging. Blowing her smoke straight at the camera, she frankly defies western notions of femininity while at the same time projecting a strong maternal image. A gender reading might say that these women represented the backbone of the post-colonial society: strong, unconventional, coolly competent.[33]

After emancipation the region became politically unstable inviting American hegemony and intervention. Between 1908–10, the United States shadowed Cuba's political administration. In 1915, after an intimidating gunboat exercise off the coast of Haiti, the Americans eventually occupied the island. In the face of this 'guardianship', images such as *Haitian Soldiers* (cat.20) reflect the self-determination in Haiti's history. Taken just weeks after yet another coup,[34] the motley military crew pose informally outside their barracks. Dressed in a way that defies the term 'uniform', they are fitted shabbily but complete. An ironic combination of pride and poverty. If resistance is registered in this image, it is in the ease that these soldiers face the viewer, totally unselfconscious and seemingly unaware of the savage stereotype the world placed on the Haitian military since the country's revolution.

The poster beside these soldiers announcing the inauguration of newly appointed president Antoine Simone,[35] places the photograph at a specific moment in history and defies the notion of the an idyllic, timeless and anonymous space so often imposed on Caribbean islands. Similarly, in another photograph, *The Cathedral* (cat.19), landmark of catholicism in Haiti, dominates the cityscape, even while under construction. That image is now an important visual document for the city of Port Au Prince,[36] since no others of the cathedral at this stage are believed to exist. In contrast to this image of orthodox religion, *Entrance of a Vudu Shrine* (cat.40) informs the viewer about Haiti's diversity. This shrine is devoted to the worship of the voodoo spirit Legba. But true to this assimilationist culture, the shrine of this African deity is decorated with imagery rooted in a European vernacular. Images of the white colonialists are juxtaposed with angels from a catholic hierarchy, surrounded by icons and imagery from the voodoo pantheon. These paintings suggest a history that is fluid, accommodating, integrated and ever present.

Numerous photographs in Johnston's archive depict the Caribbean as a place of development and modernity. The market scenes of Haiti teem with energy, bearing all the signs of a frontier town hurtling towards urbanisation. Men, women and donkeys walk with a sense of urgency against the backdrop of the recently imported iron market and the new tram lines. Similarly, Trinidad and Barbadian images of market women reflect a new kind of vending and the separation of town from country.[37]

Modernity is registered even in the images of the countryside. In Jamaica and Cuba, we see evidence of sugar, tobacco and banana industries. The two images *Negroes at Work* (cat.49) and *Cuban Negroes at Play* (cat.48) indicate voluntary migration and regional integration. The subjects, most likely migrant job-workers from Haiti and Jamaica, convey the camaraderie between these economically motivated islanders who after 1850, worked alongside each other in the cane fields of Cuba and on the railway and construction sites of Panama,[38] Haiti, Honduras, Costa Rica, and Nicaragua.

Johnston's trip brought a paradigm shift in his assessment of blacks. Even as he was writing *Negro in the New World* his views appeared to be changing. Johnston's tour of the New World also seems to have been a catalyst for later ethnographic and anthropological work where the Negro is viewed as a potential partner for the European rather than the 'white man's burden.' After the 1914 War, Johnston regularly wrote about the white man's responsibility to other races, the possibility of self-government for blacks, and the relationship between all races.[39] His tone changed from the condescending Bwana one finds in his assessment of Africans to that of a partner who can gain from the history and pathos of those who didn't look like him.

Johnston used his camera prolifically and judiciously to record the development of Afro-Caribbeans under colonialism. Technically, and as a research tool, it suited his purpose. Artistically, it satisfied his discerning eye for anecdotal and poignant images. Academically and professionally, it articulated a thousand times better than his writing could convey. These images are successful because they give his ideas currency today, when they might be better understood. Johnston predicted that one day black people would smile tolerantly at the crude theories of a white man like himself and consider them quaint.[40] While his approach to racial issues may now be outdated, the images Johnston left us are not. There is still much to learn from *Photos and Phantasms*. In this exhibition, we can recognise ourselves and others inside and outside of these frames.

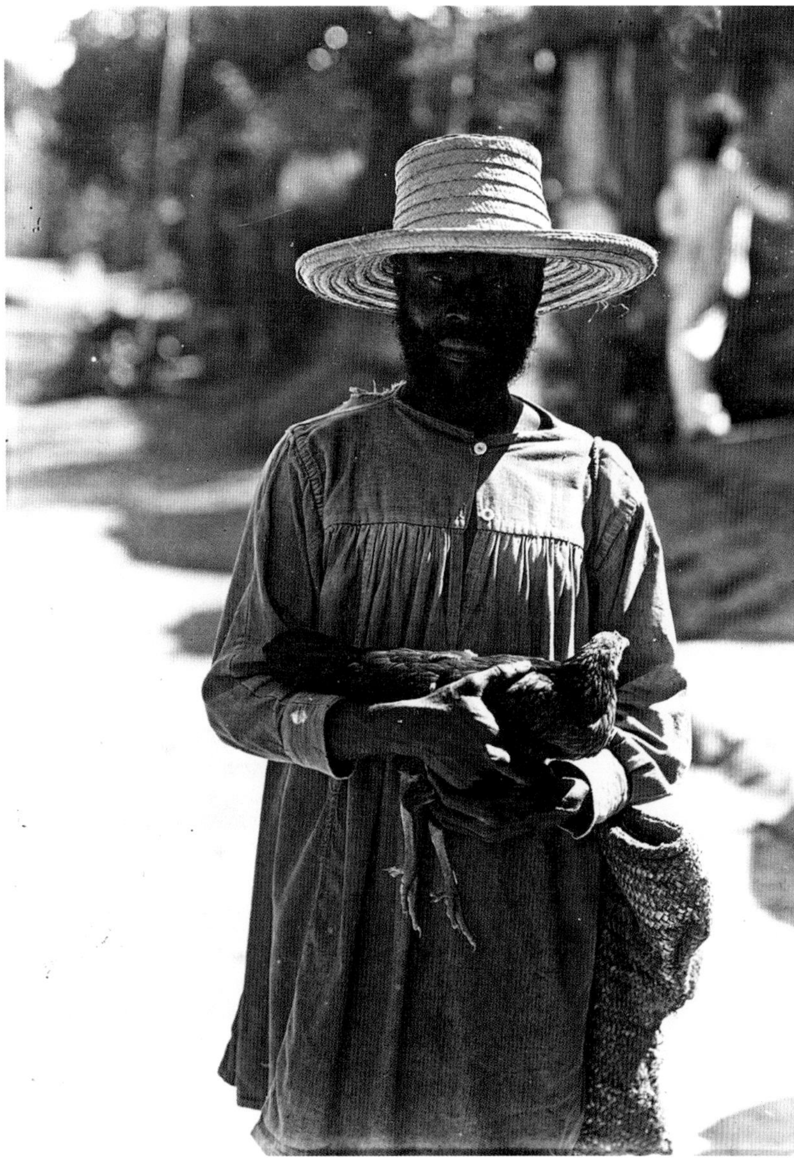

Haitian Peasant, Haiti *cat.2*

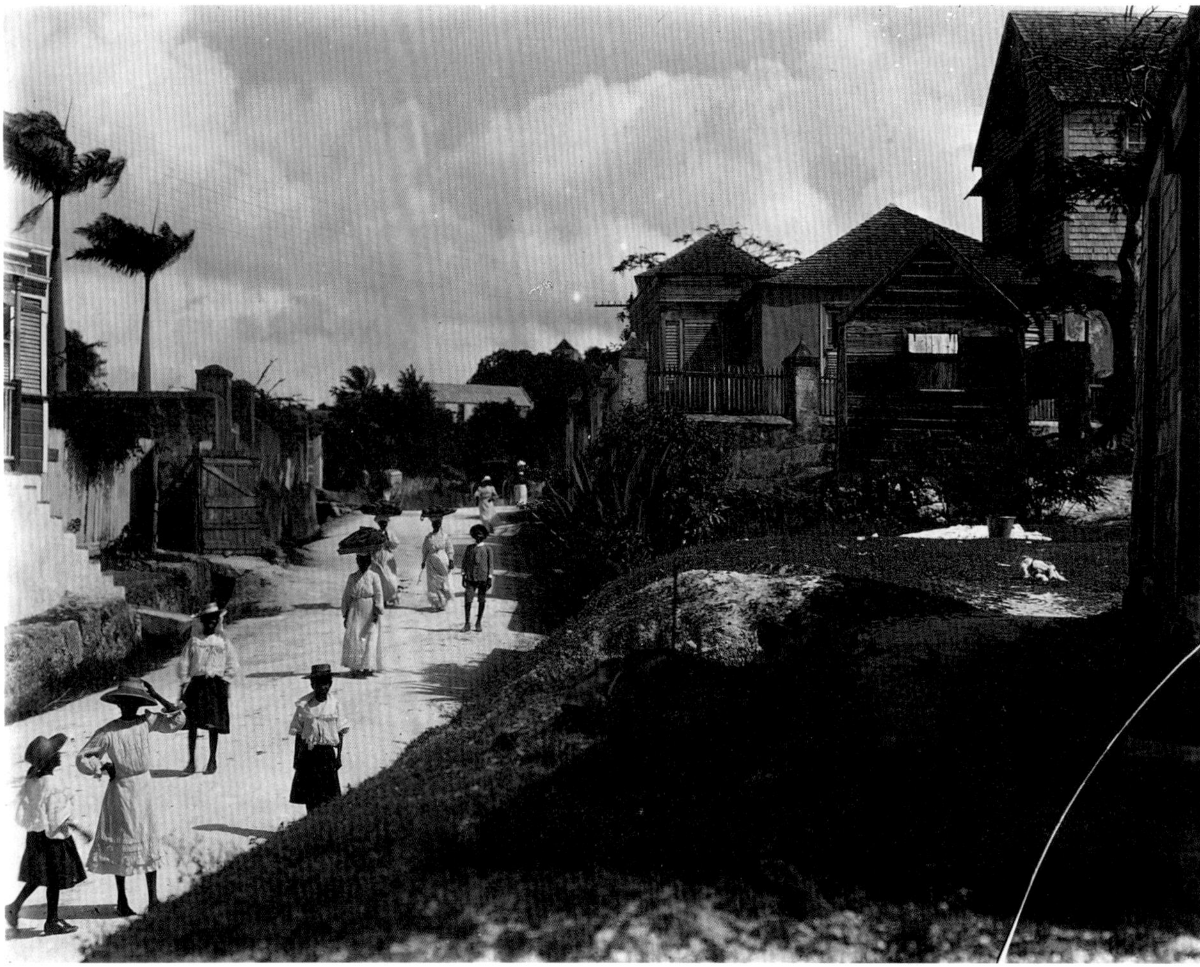

A Road Outwards, the Country, Barbados *cat.57*

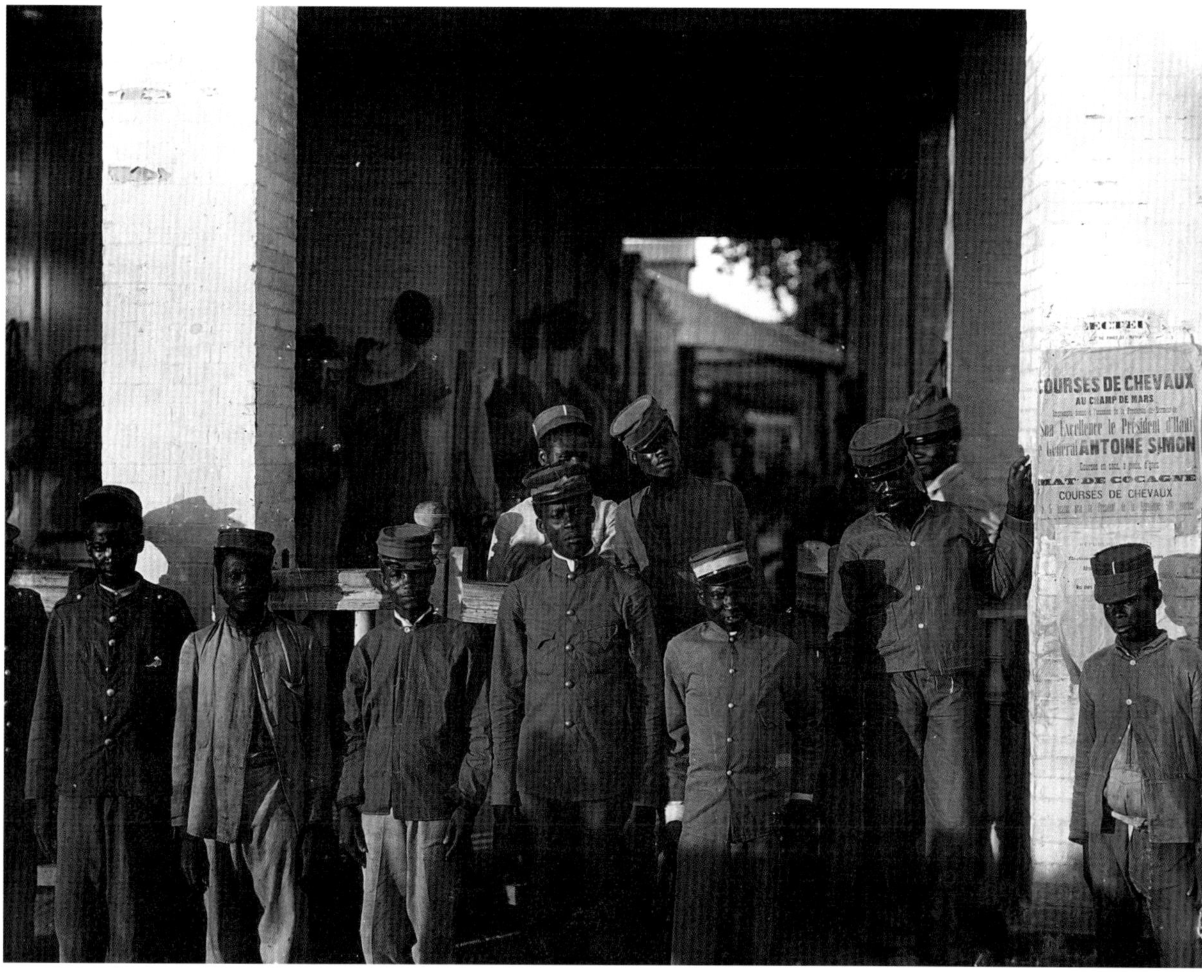

Haitian Soldiers, Haiti *cat.20*

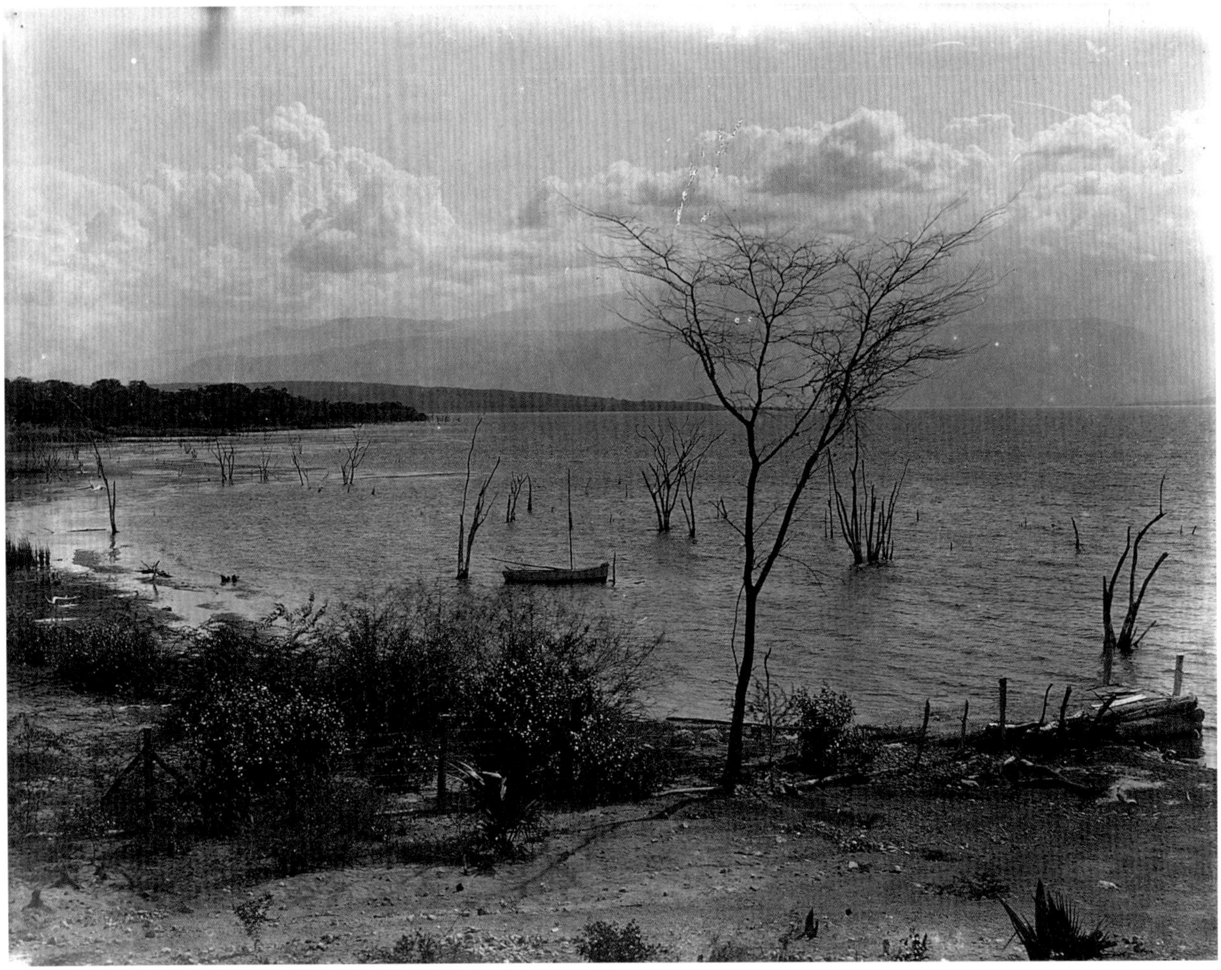

above Lake Azuey, San Domingo, Dominican Republic *cat.24*
right Haitian Woman with Children, Haiti *cat.25*

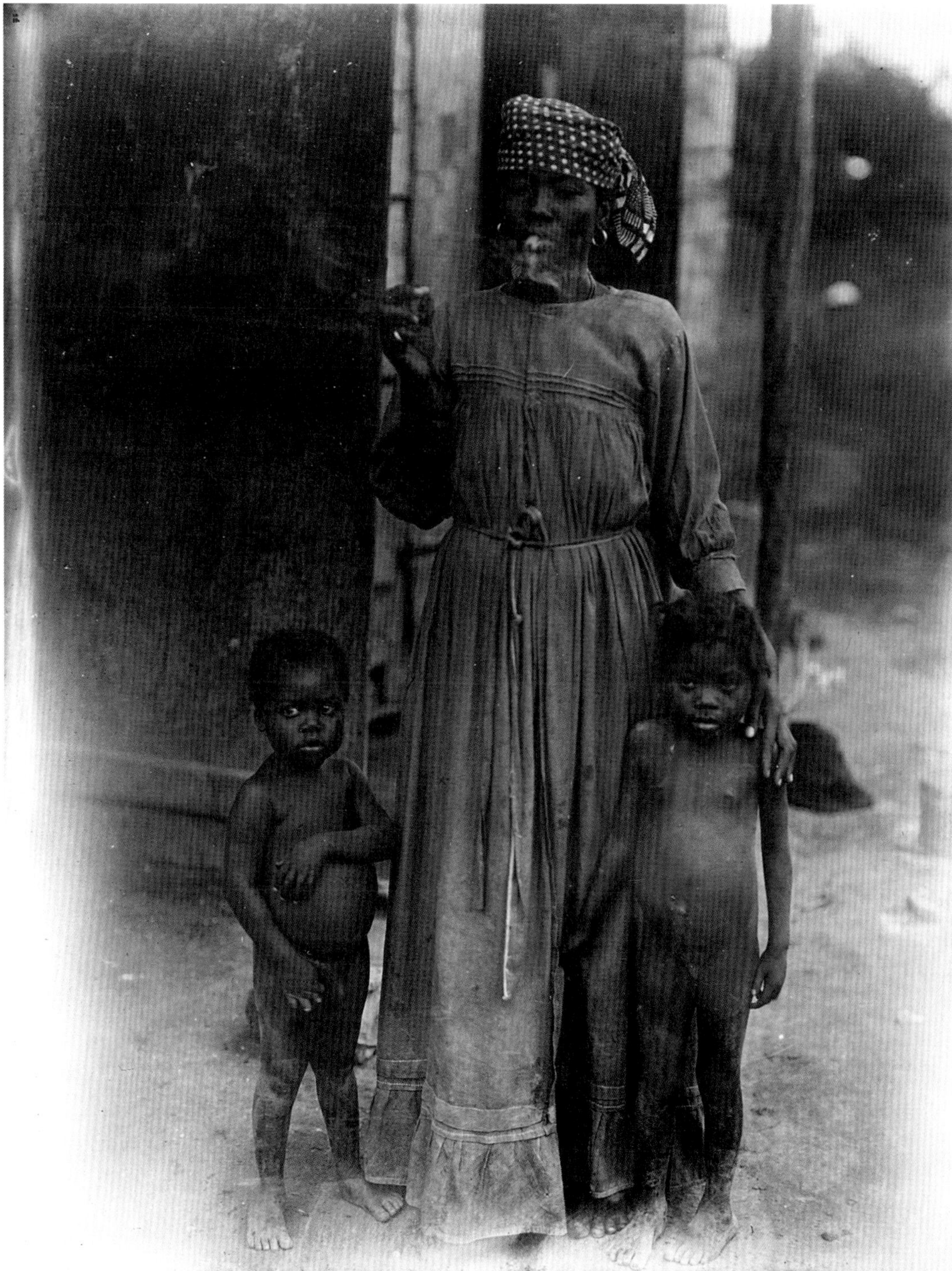

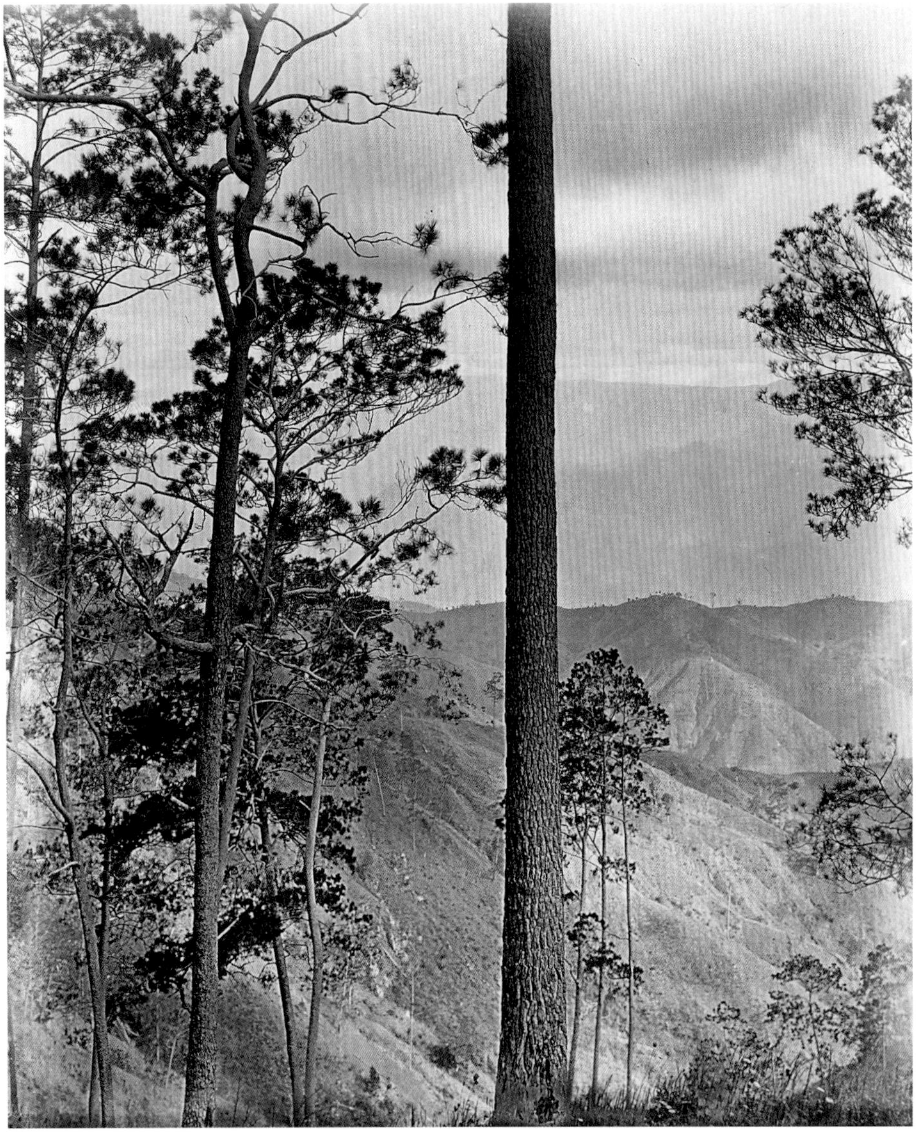

above Haitian Mountains *cat.34*
right Entrance of a Vudu Shrine, Haiti *cat.39*

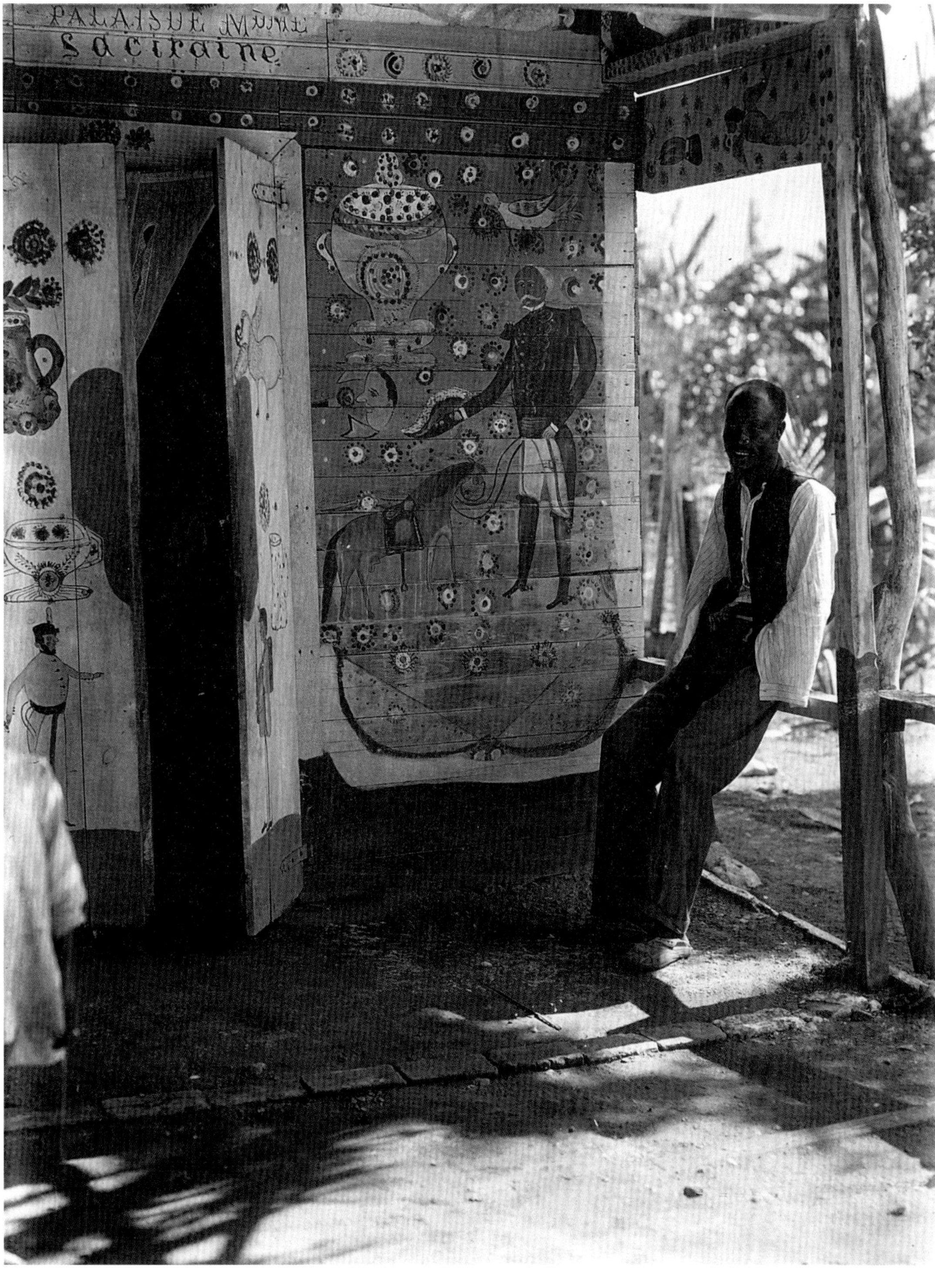
PALAISDE Mme
Lacitaine

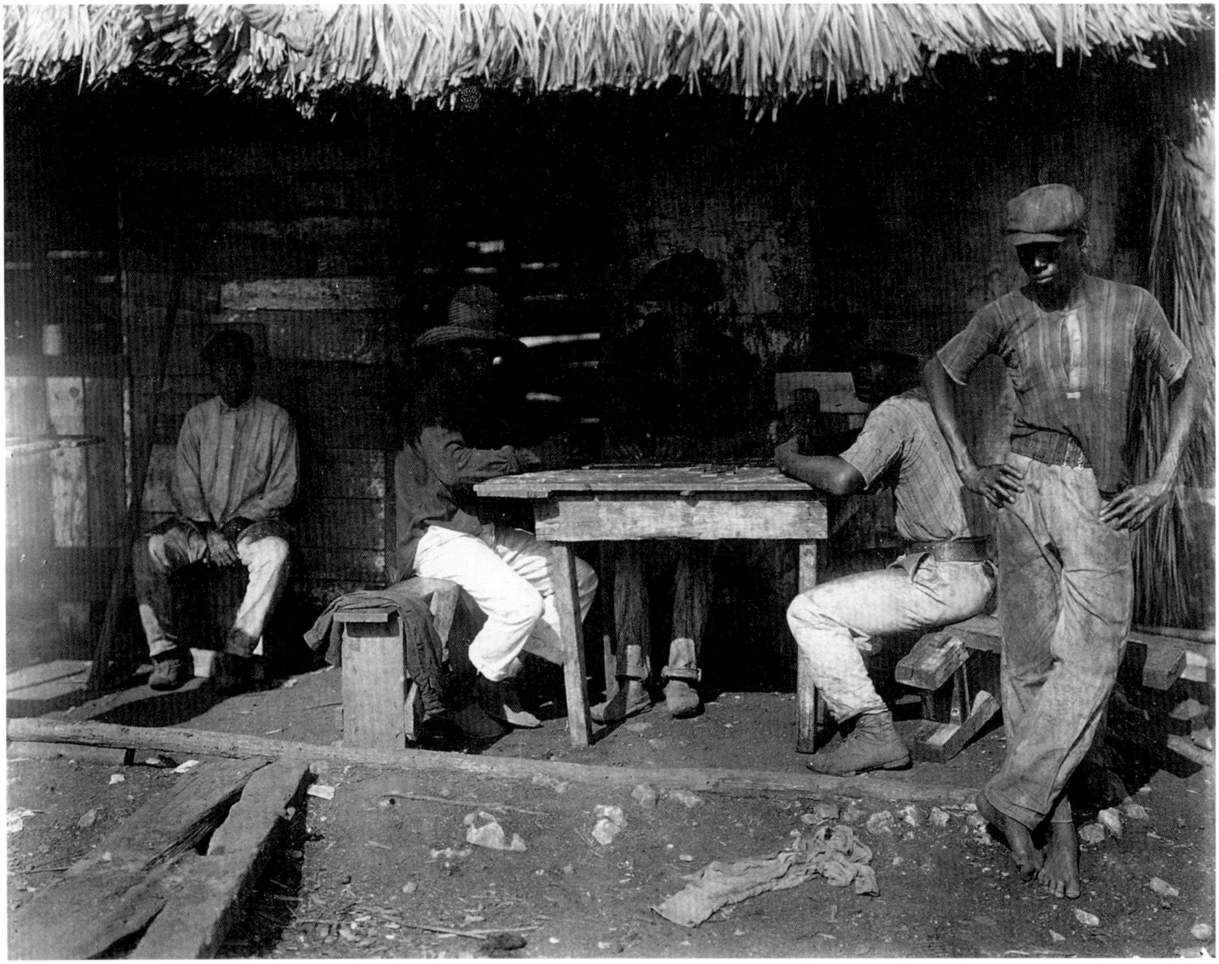

Cuban Negroes at Play, Cuba *cat.48*

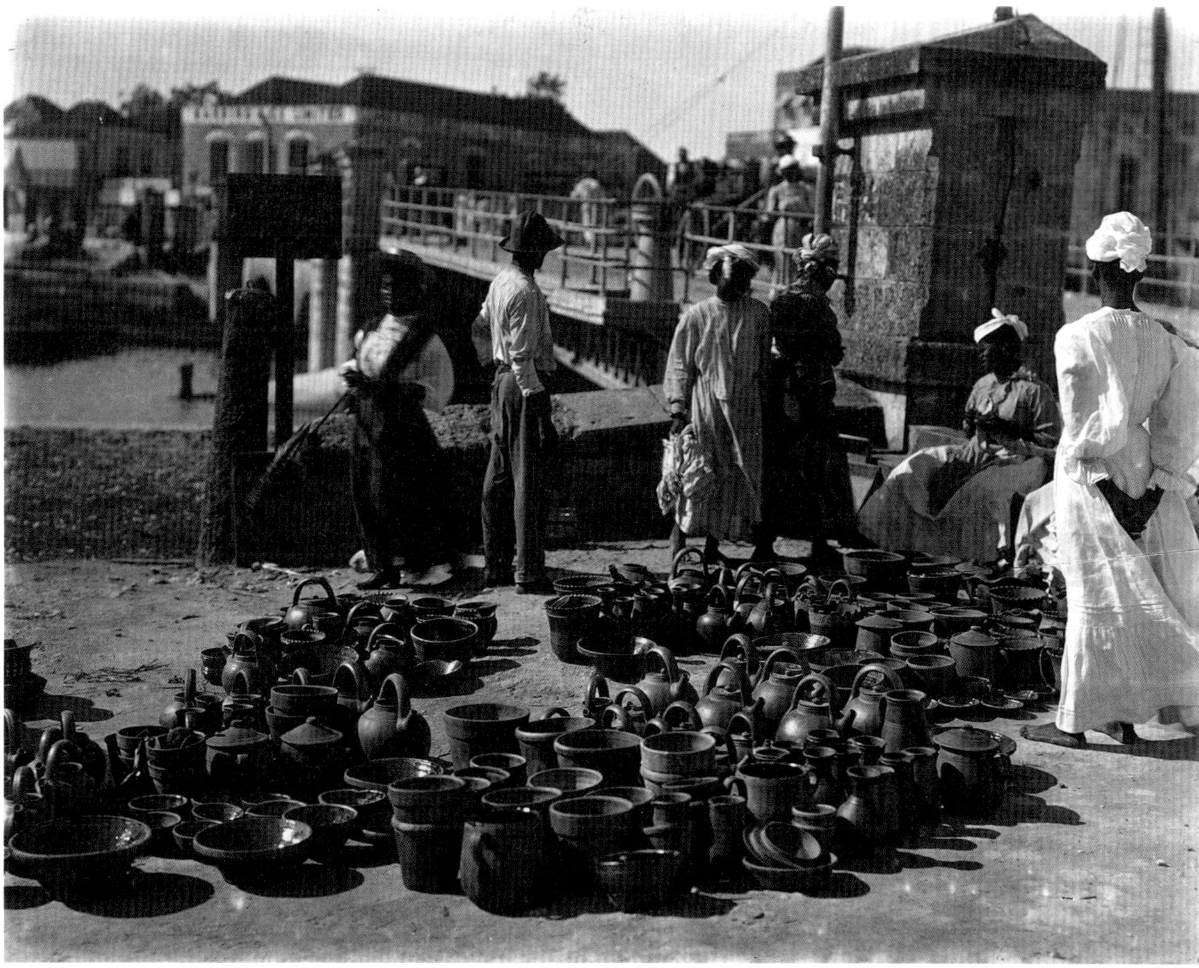

Negro Pottery, Barbados *cat.62*

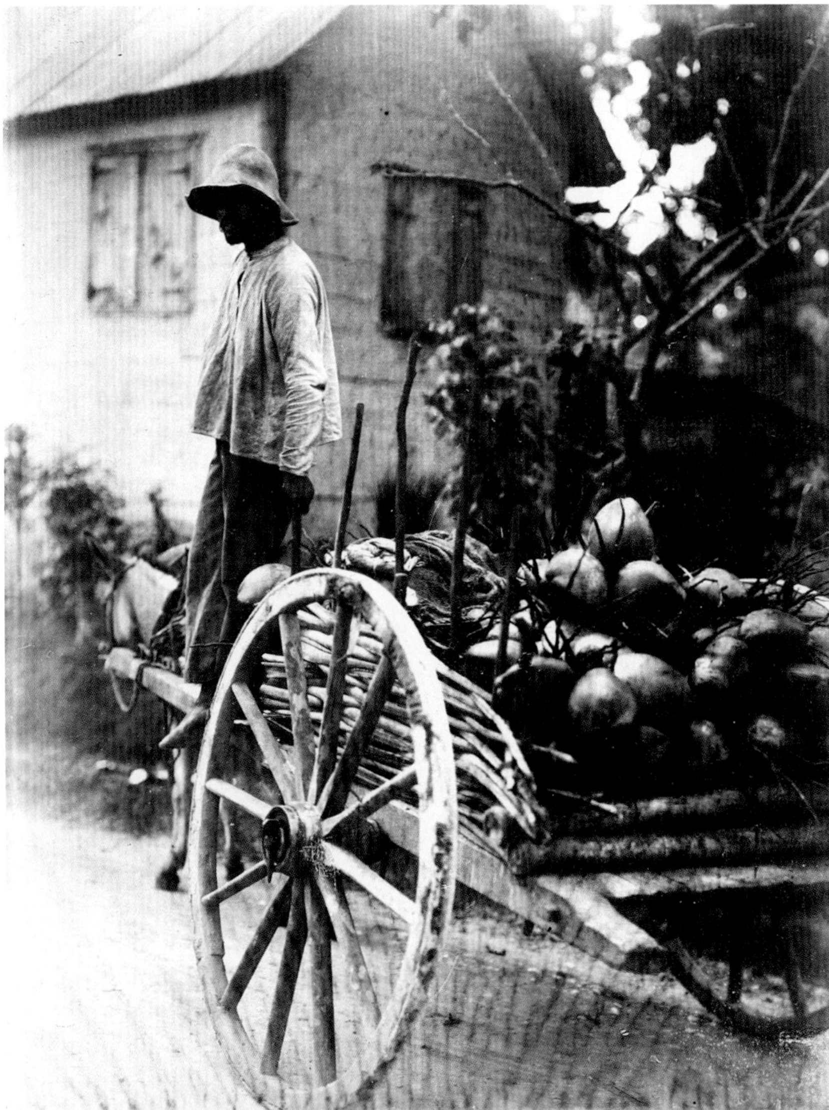

above Unripe Coconuts, Trinidad *cat.69*
right A Woman Selling Jack Fruit, Trinidad *cat.68*

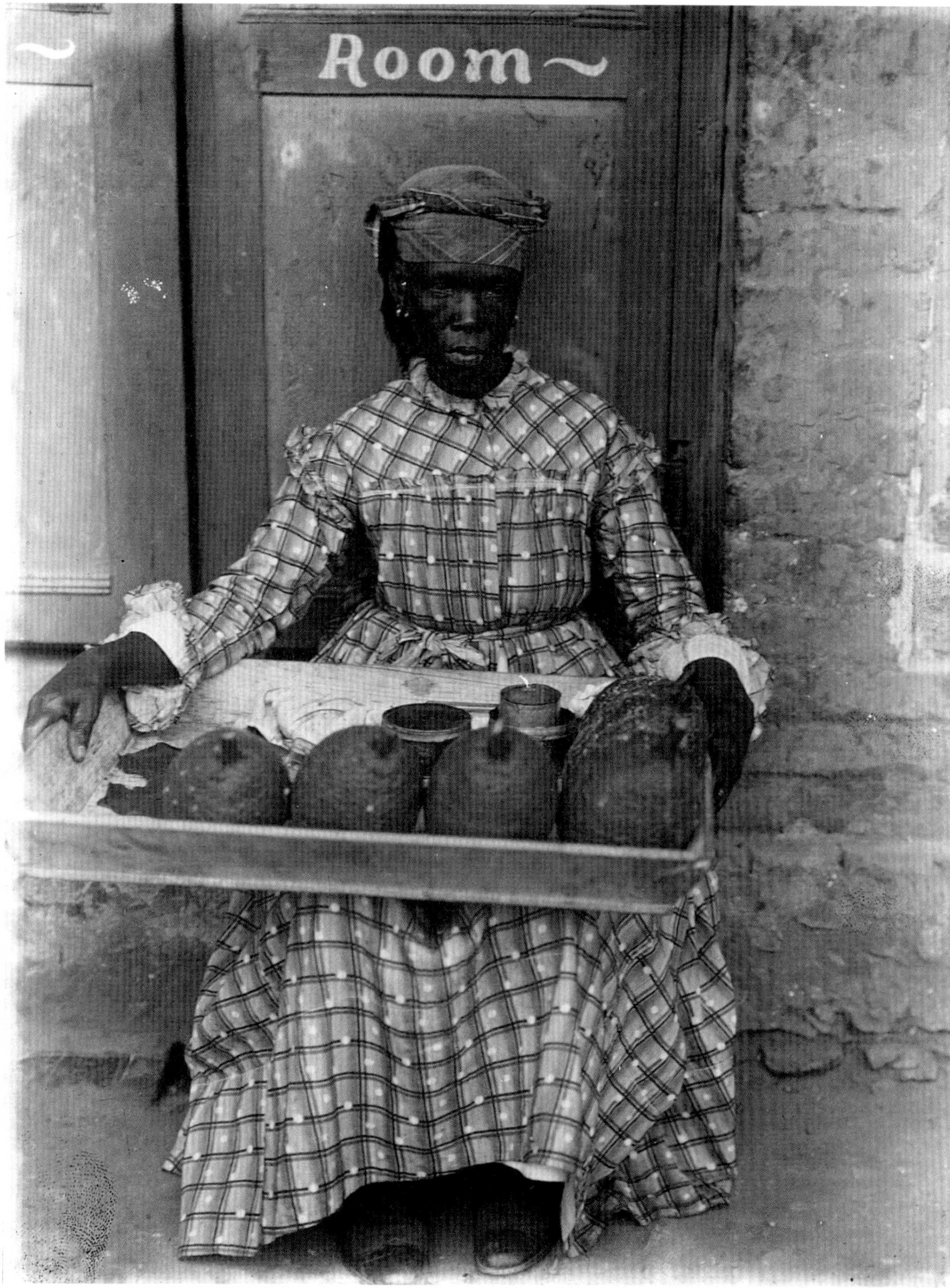
Room~

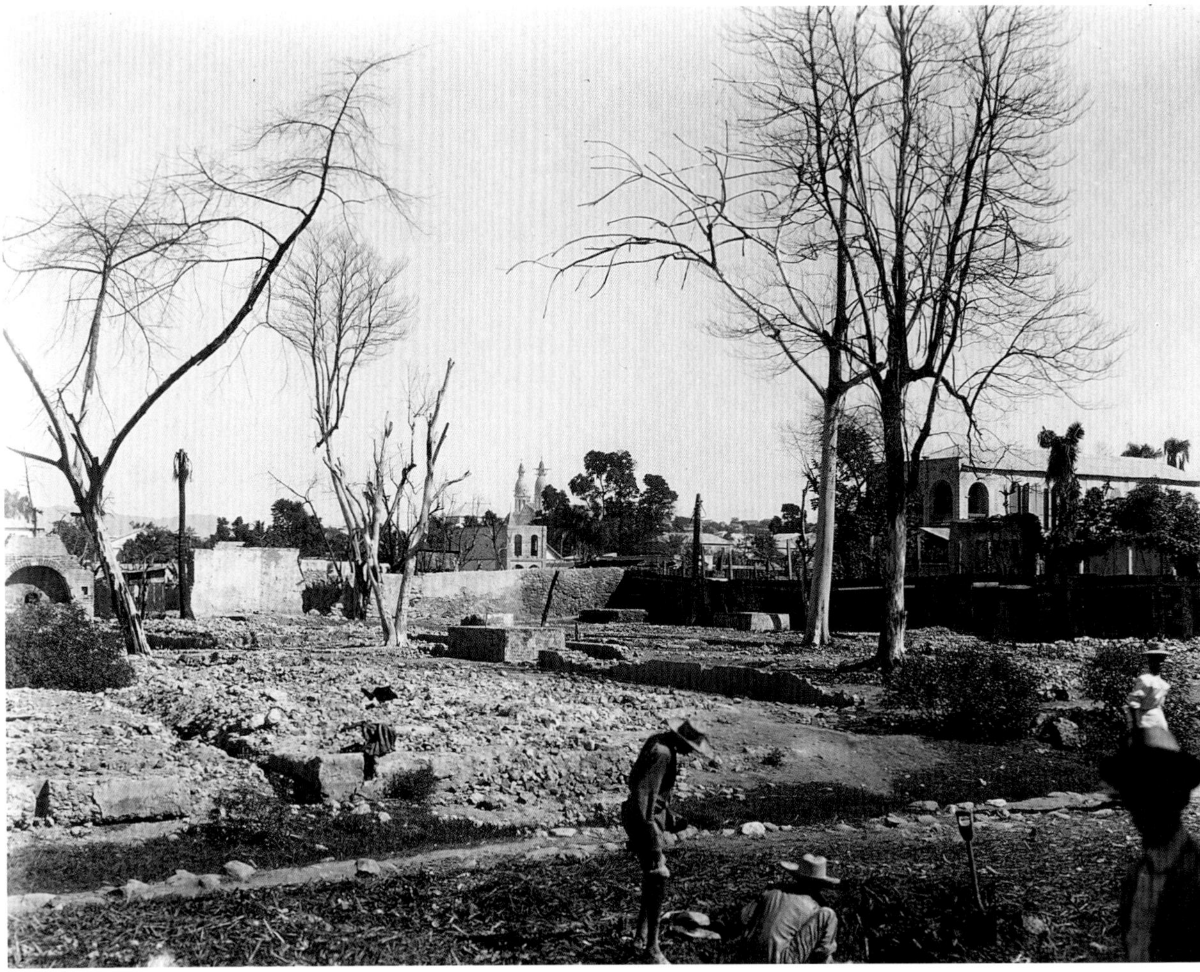

above Burial Master, West Port au Prince, Haiti *cat.17*
right An Agave: Lake Shore, Haiti *cat.28*

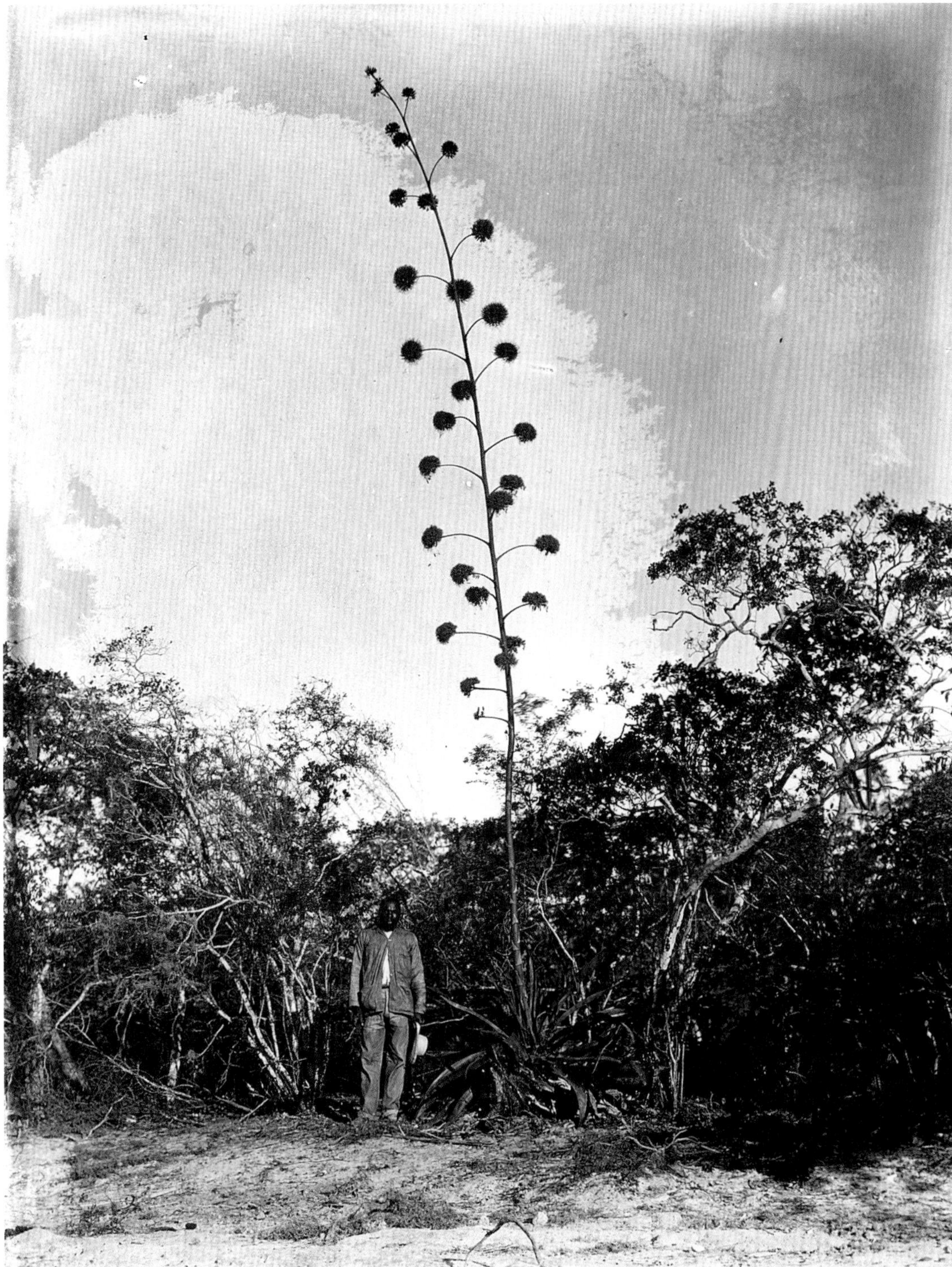

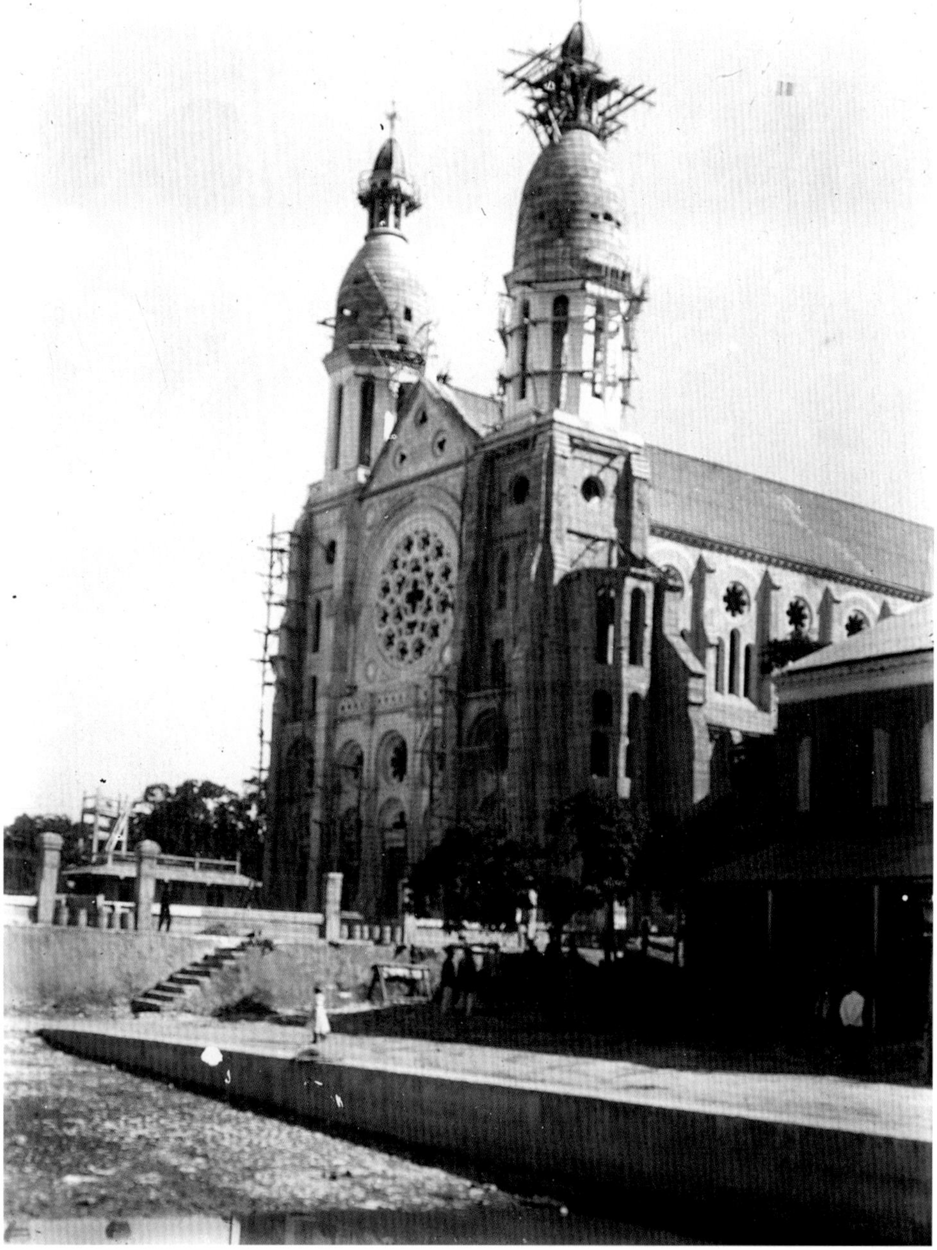

The Cathedral, Port au Prince, Haiti *cat.19*

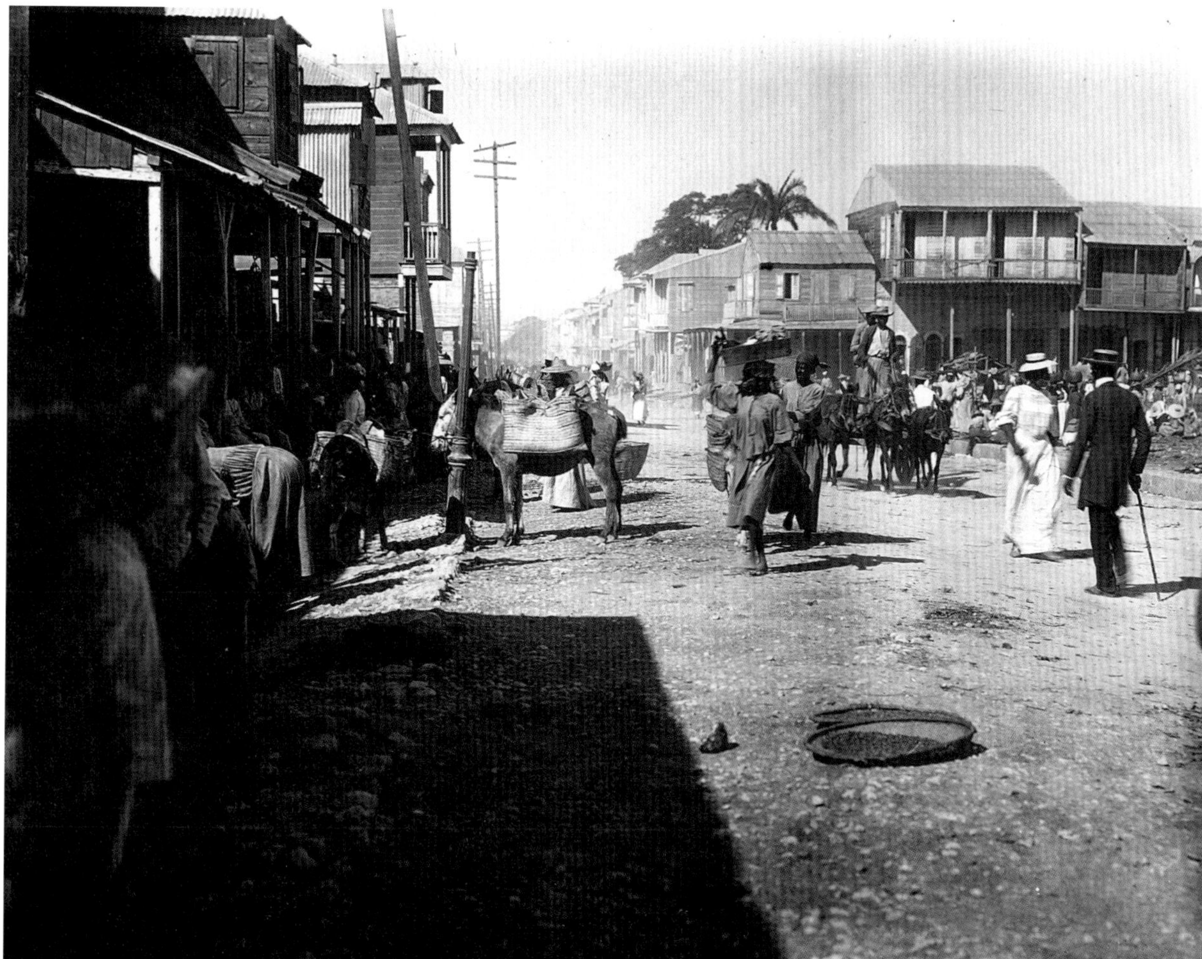

A Market Place, Port au Prince, Haiti *cat.18*

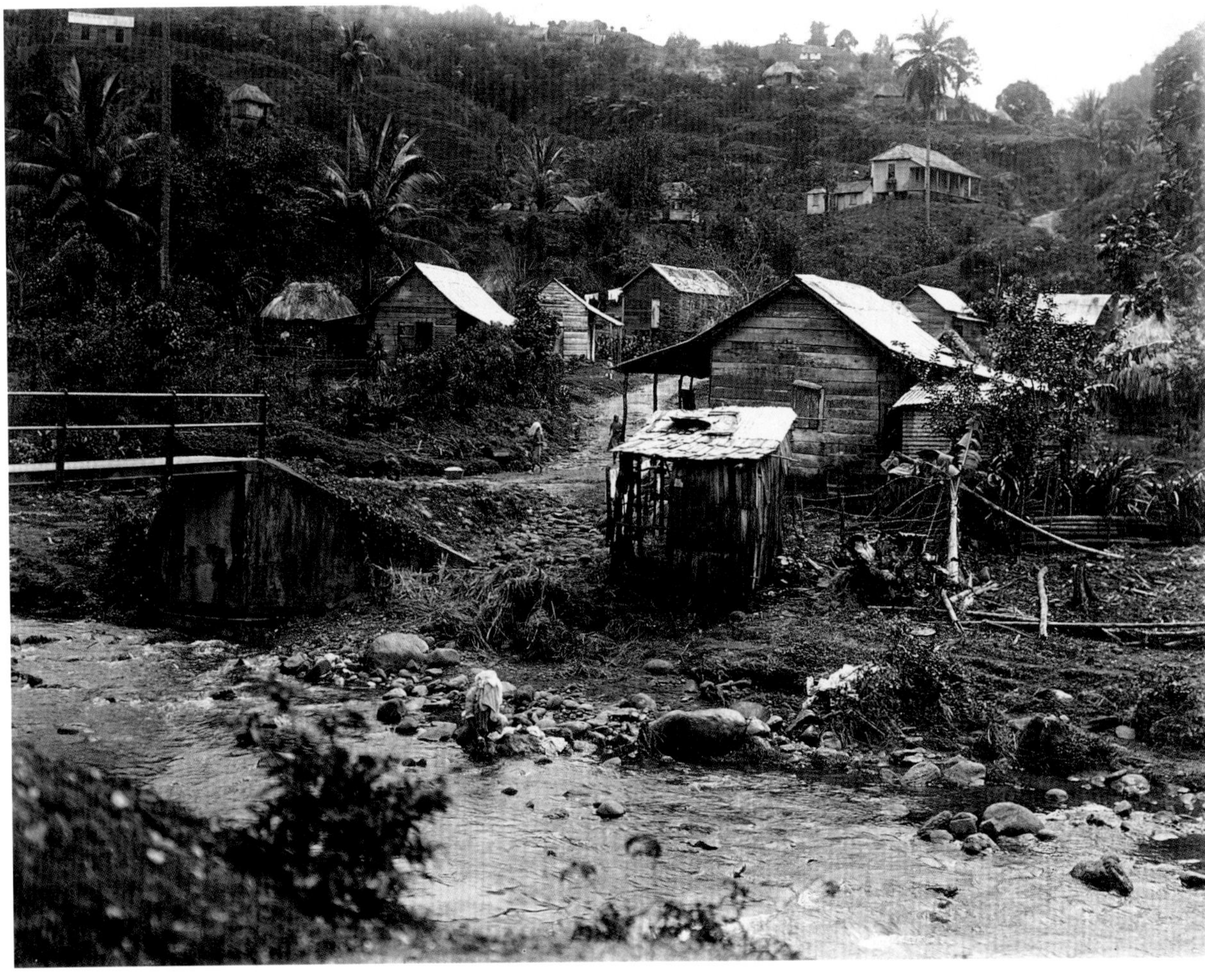

above In the Maroon Country, Jamaica *cat.53*
right Negroes at Work, Cuba *cat.49*

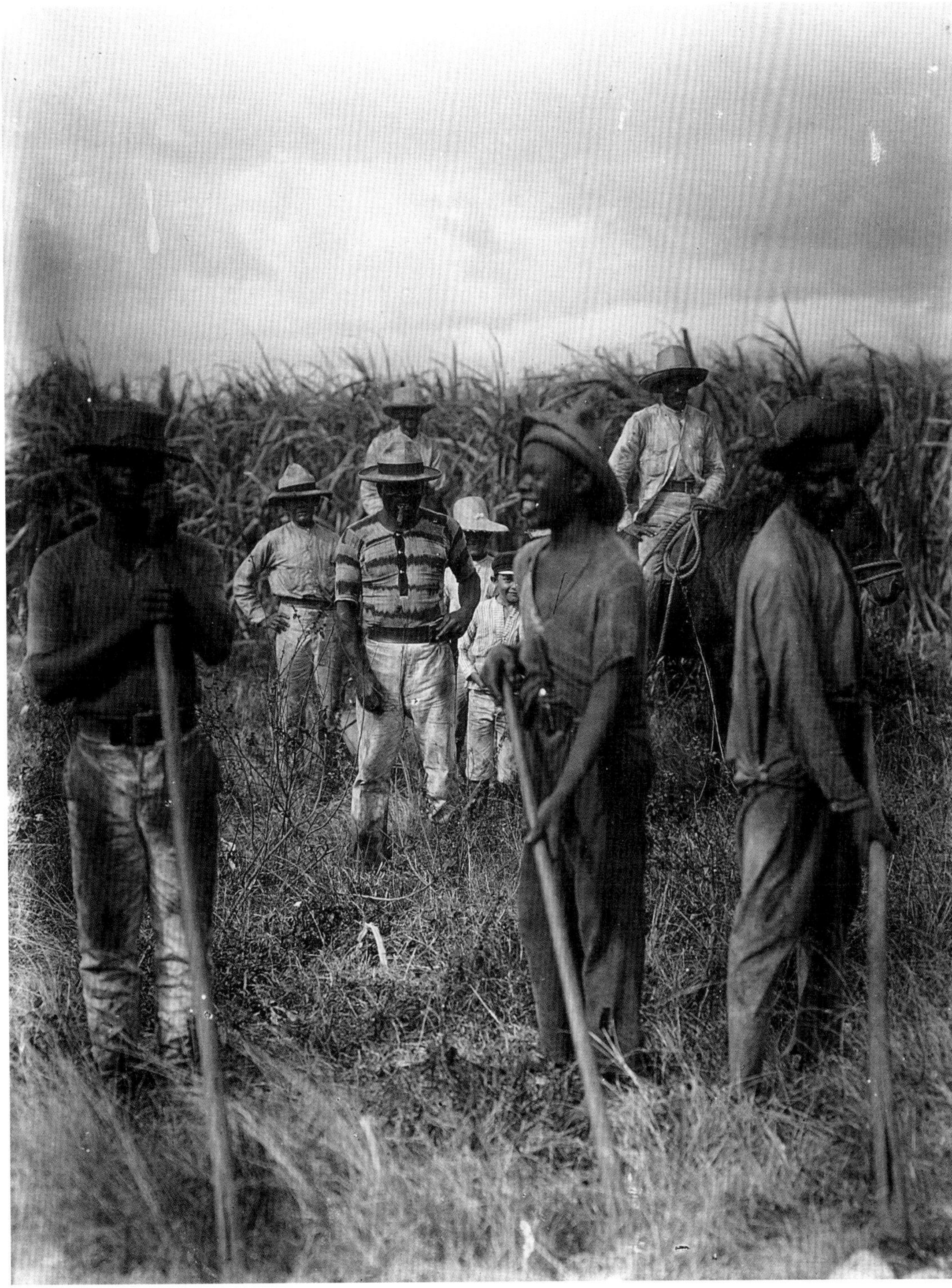

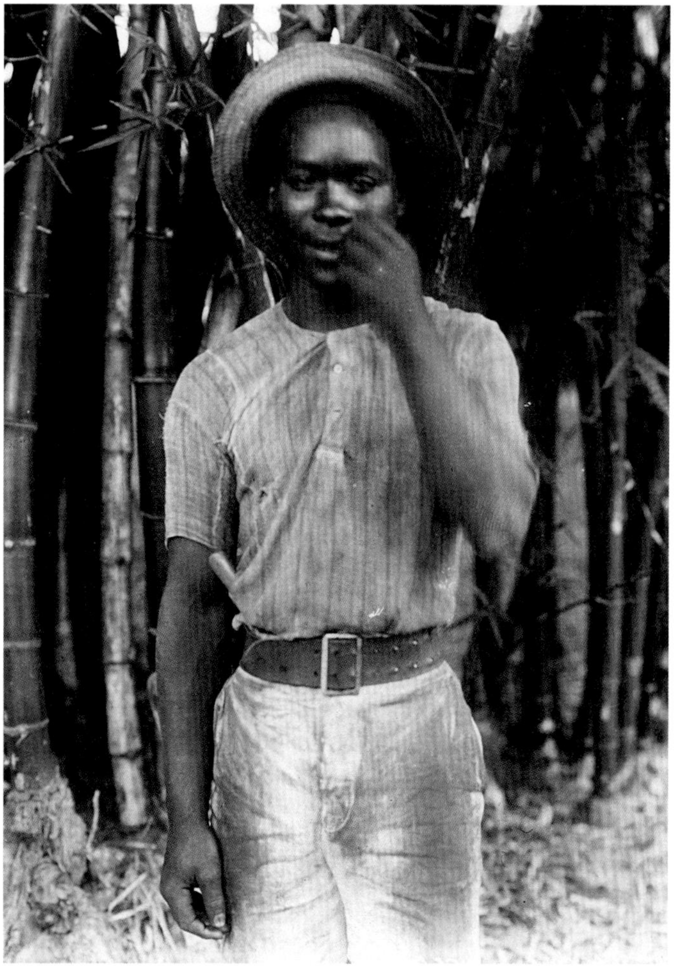

A Cuban Negro *cat.7*

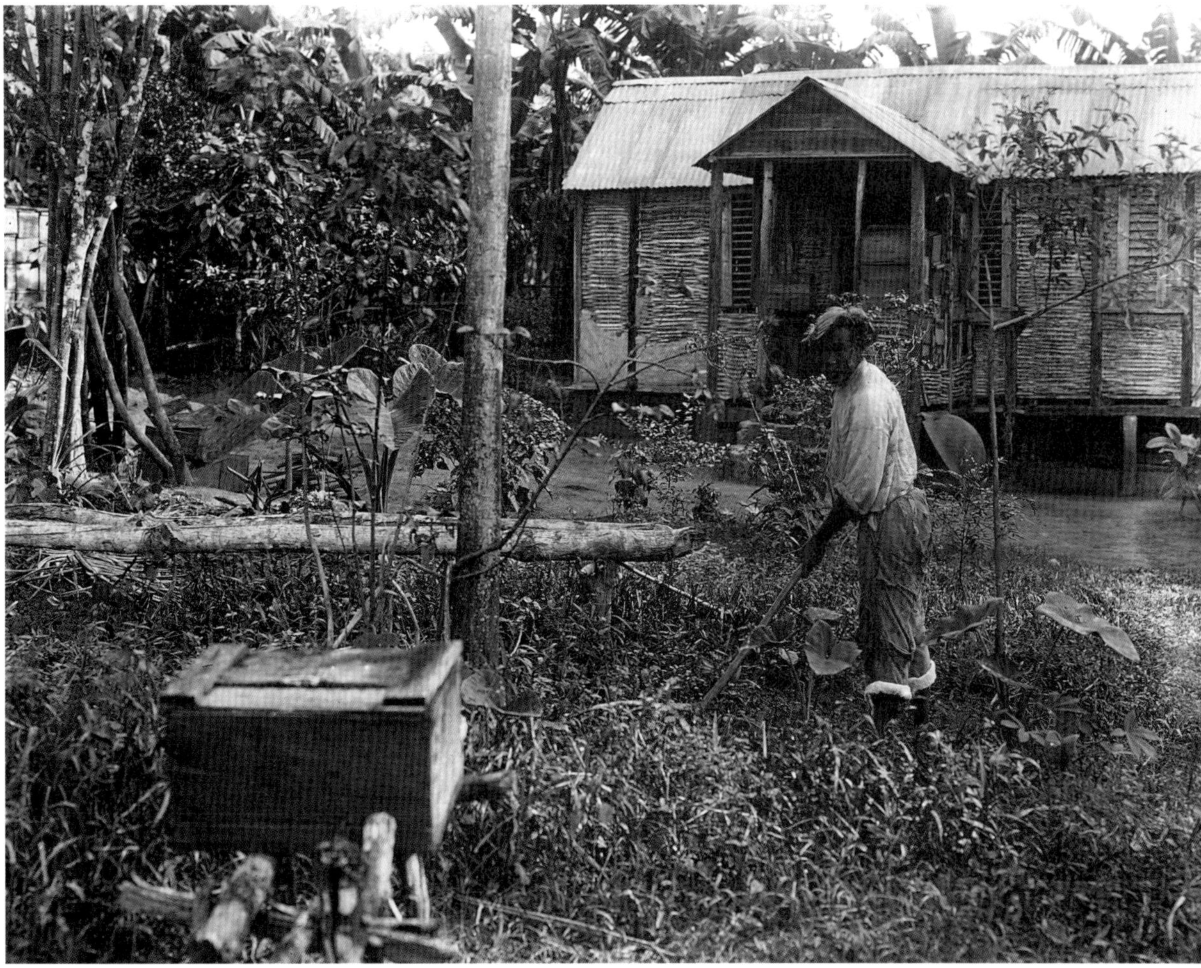

A Jamaican Farmer or Beekeeper *cat.37*

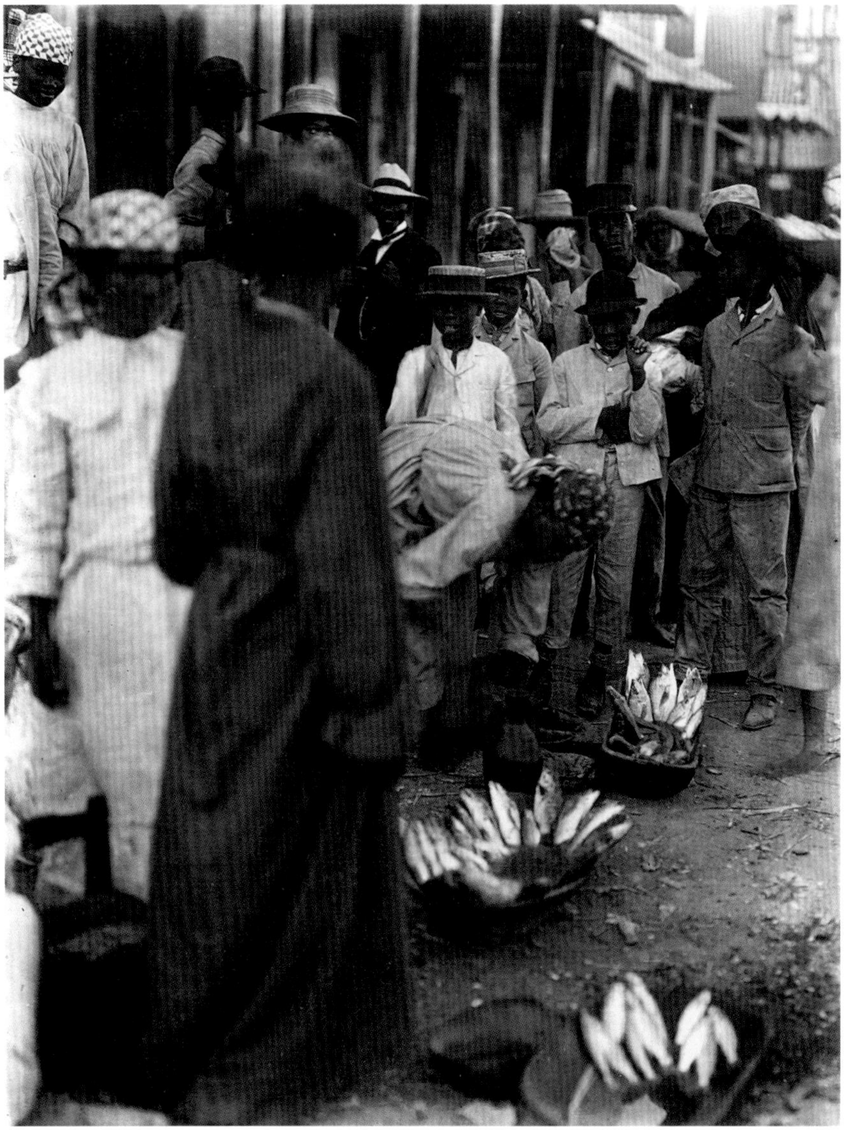

above A Market of Fish, Port au Prince, Haiti *cat.45*
right Street in Port Maria / Road in Jamaica *cat.66*

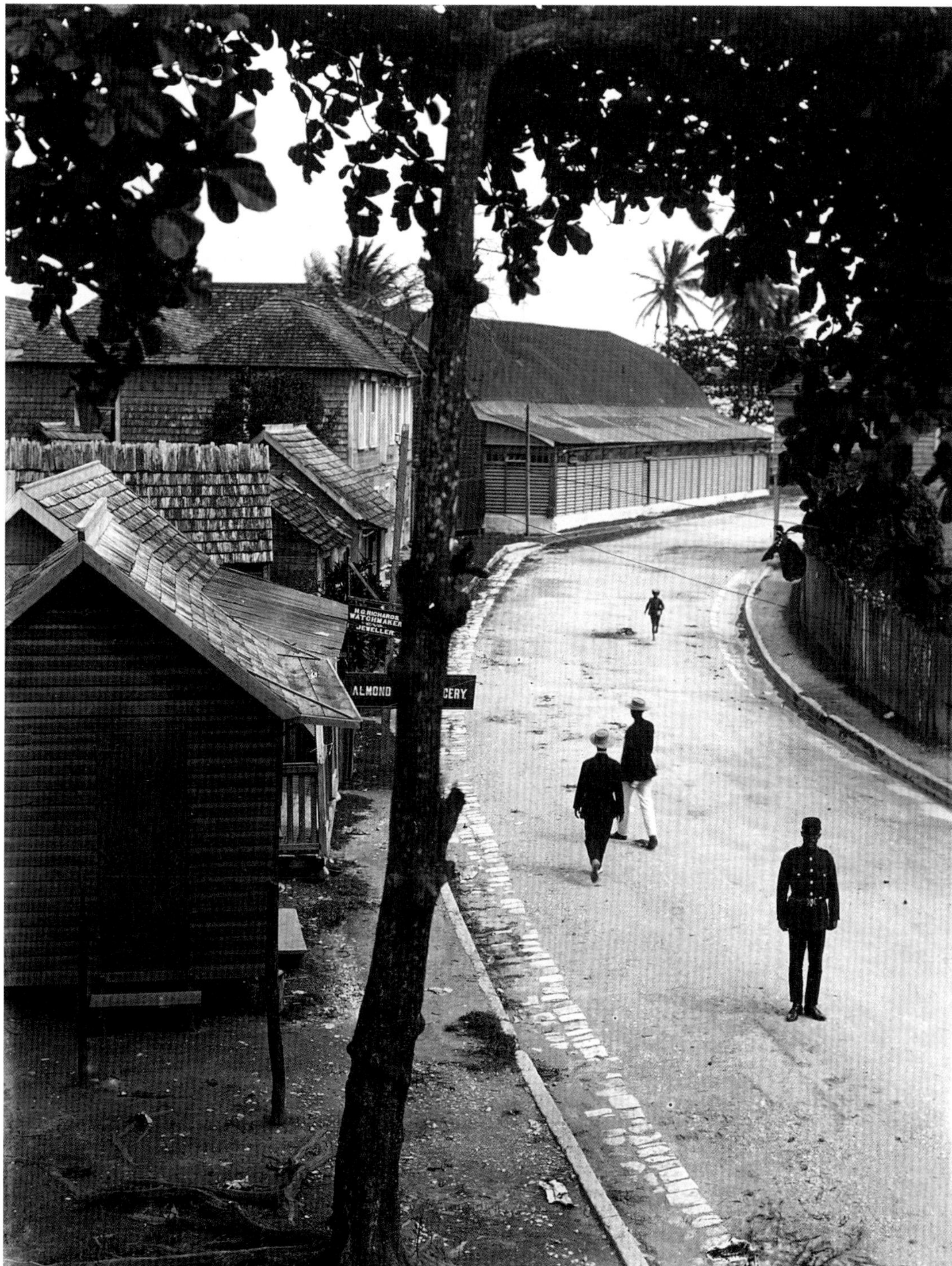
H.G. RICHARDS
WATCHMAKER
JEWELLER
ALMOND
CERY.

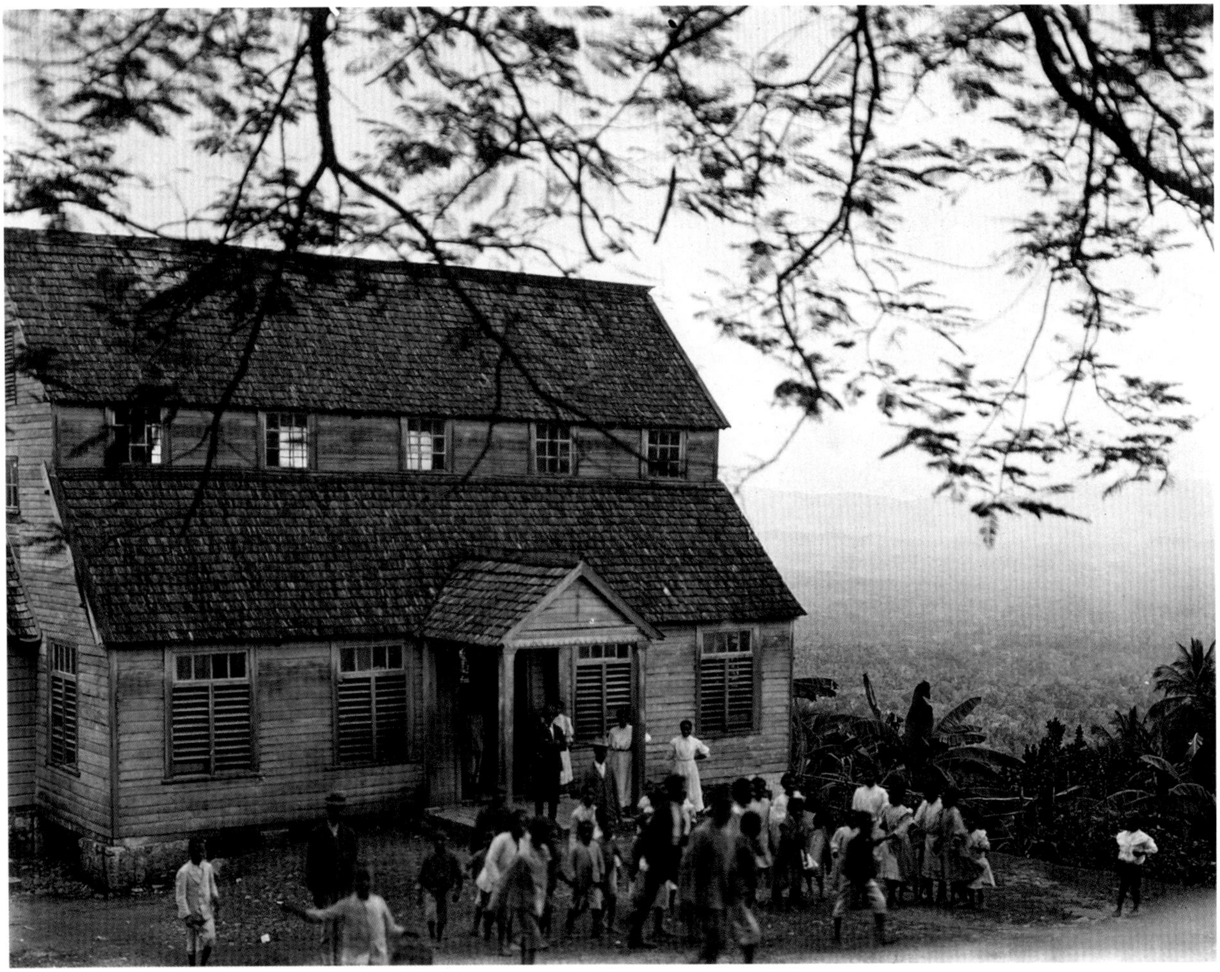

above A Country School, Jamaica *cat.33*
right In Port Maria, Jamaica *cat.54*

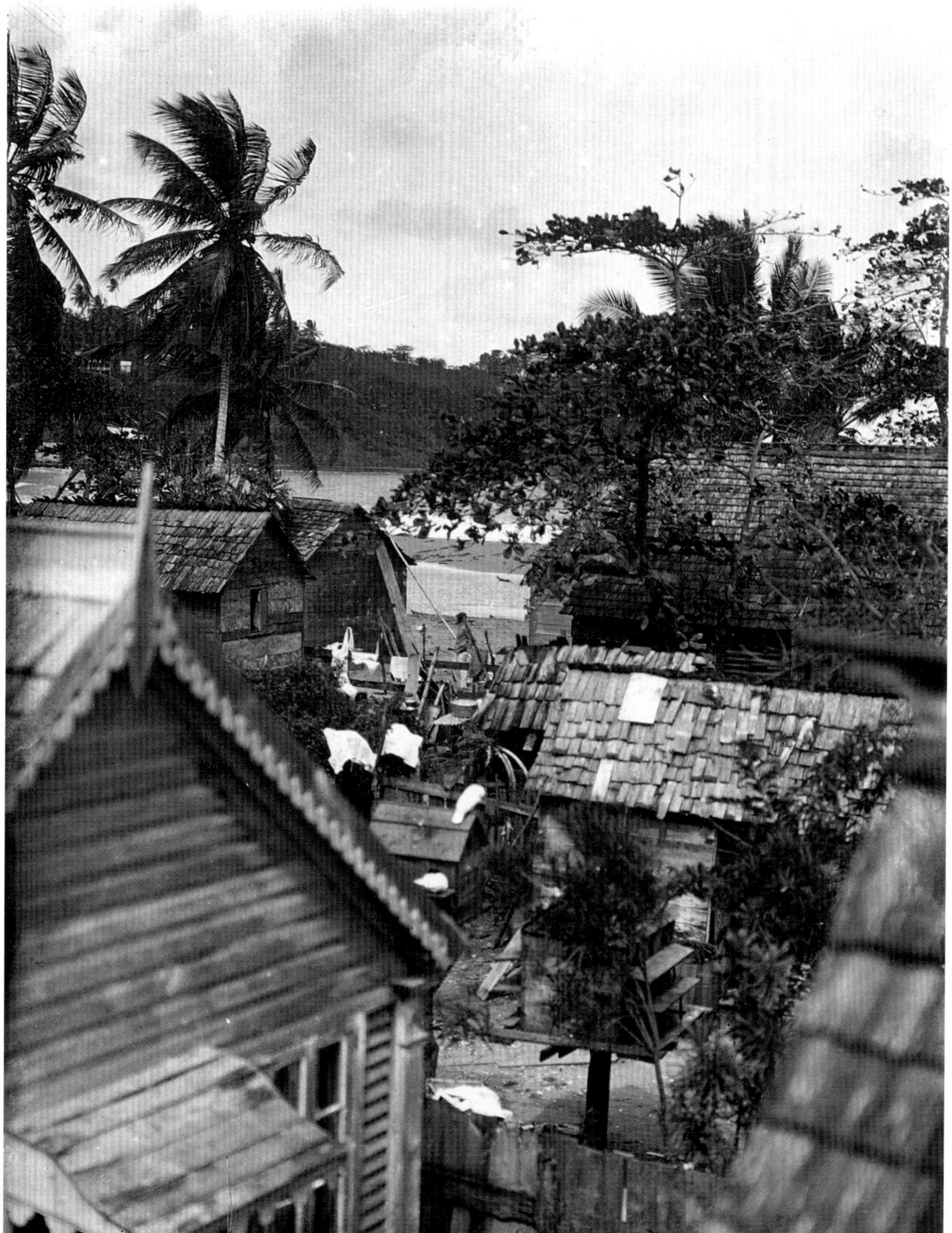

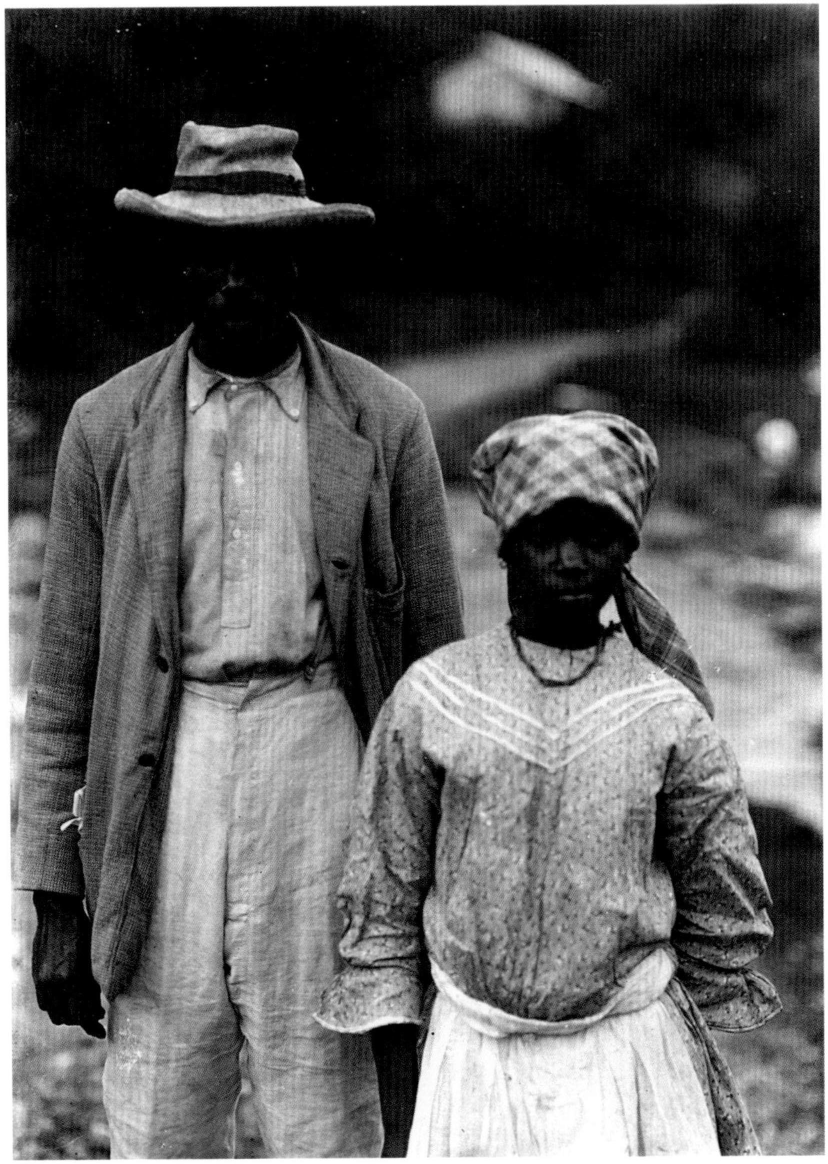

Maroon Negroes, Jamaica *cat.9*

Harry Johnston's Photographs of the Caribbean

Catalogue

The titles of the photographs are derived from Harry Johnston's own captions. The number at the foot of each entry is the original reference number for his glass plate negatives.

* An asterisk indicates a photograph illustrated in the plate section.

1
The Market, Port au Prince
Haiti

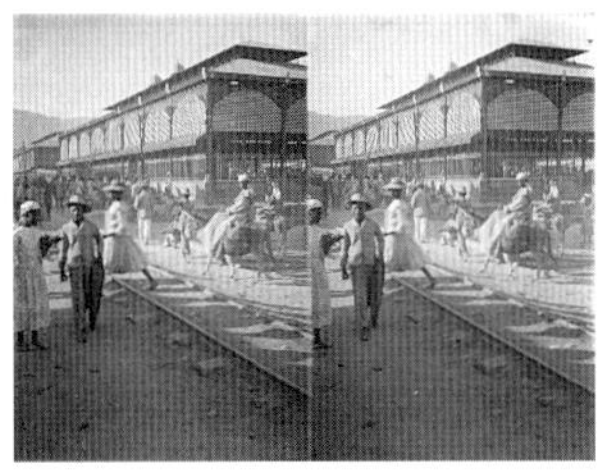

The *marche en fer*, (iron market) or *Marche Vallières*, was made in France and shipped to Haiti in 1897. A Turkish design complete with minaret, it had become the centre of trade and commerce in Port au Prince at the time of Johnston's visit. He records that the heat and smells inside made trading outside more comfortable. The tramway served this thoroughfare with a limited service from the Champ de Mars to the Rue de Quai, three kilometres away, from six in the morning until seven at night. The scene has an air of modernity, people hustle across the streets and the crowds in the distance indicate that this may have been a Saturday market.

B4434

2*
Haitian Peasant
Haiti

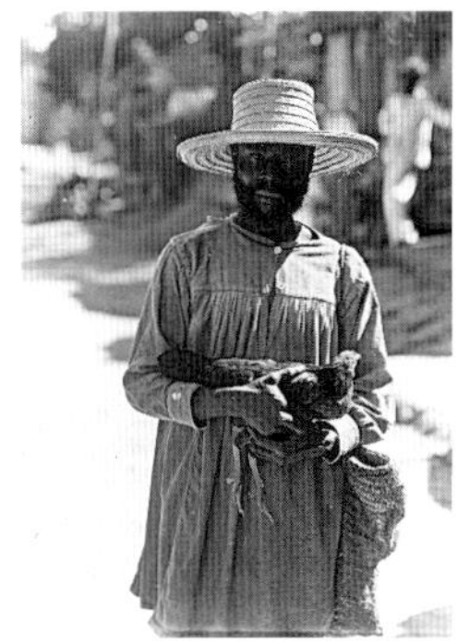

The Haitian peasant in this small glass portrait stands outside the main market in Port au Prince. Dressed in a blue chambray or *carabella* smock, typical peasant dress for men and women in this era, he holds a live hen that he will sell at the market. Live produce in the market is more typical of Haiti and other French islands. Use of the market as a place of small informal commercial trading, however, became a tradition in the Caribbean during slavery. After emancipation, it represented the possibility of economic independence and an improved standard of living.

B4436

3
Cactus House
Haiti

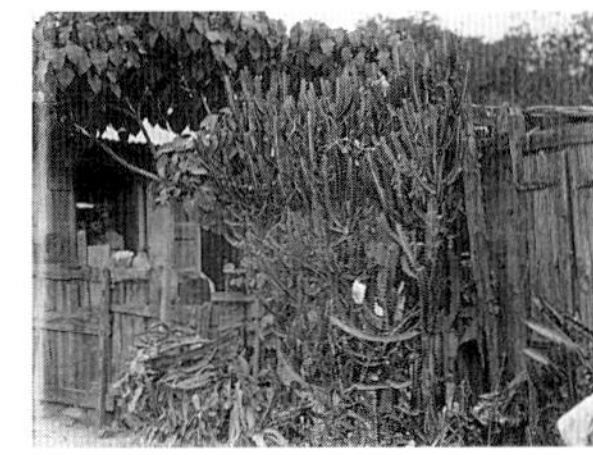

Johnston called this house covered in cactus, *'a ramshackle Haitian dwelling defended by cacti'*. Cactus of this type, *savane desolée,* was used often for fencing to keep stray animals out. This image may have been useful for Johnston's naturalist theories, to show how Caribbean people had adapted and become integrated with their environment.

B4439

4

Peasant Women

Haiti

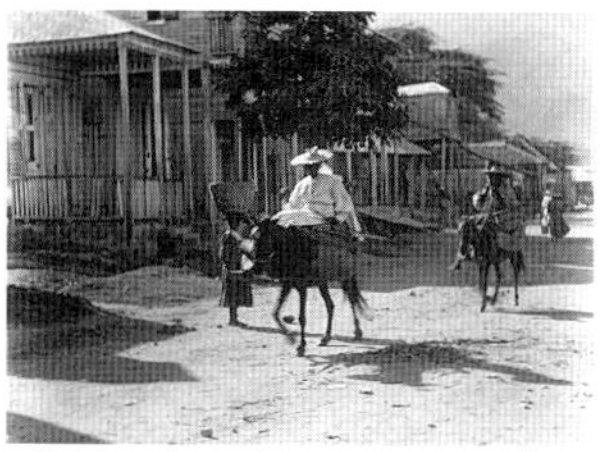

A scene dominated by women, indicating their importance as informal traders in the network of markets established during and after slavery. Two women ride donkeys saddled with *bankra* or *halfort* baskets filled with produce. The gingerbread houses lining the route into Port au Prince display a local vernacular of European origin, the wooden fretwork being substituted for popular European wrought iron designs was made in France and shipped to Haiti in 1897. Germans, who had become significant traders in the Haitian economy, built residential areas such as these.

B4440

5

A Haitian Farmer

Haiti

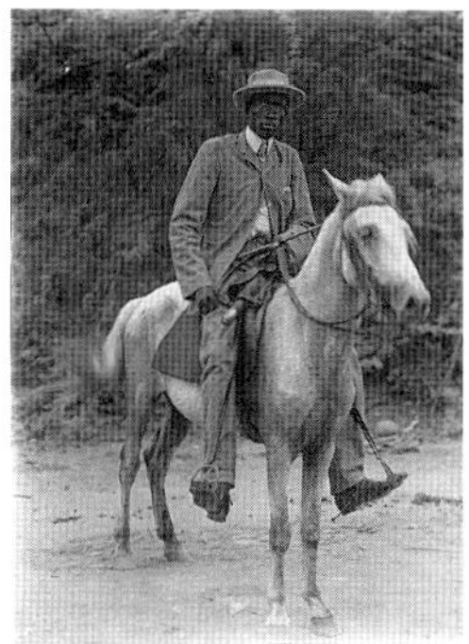

A portrait of a Haitian farmer who Johnston refers to as *'well-to-do'*. His wealth is apparent from his European styled clothing and his horse. Ownership of land became synonymous with freedom. In 1891, land was distributed to the military according to rank as a reward for service, thus creating a new class of landlords. Black men, such as this farmer, may have benefitted from the revolutionary government's attempts to redistribute land and the departure of both French planters and Haitian mulatto élite, after the Haitian Revolution in 1804.

B4447

6

Royal Palms

Cuba

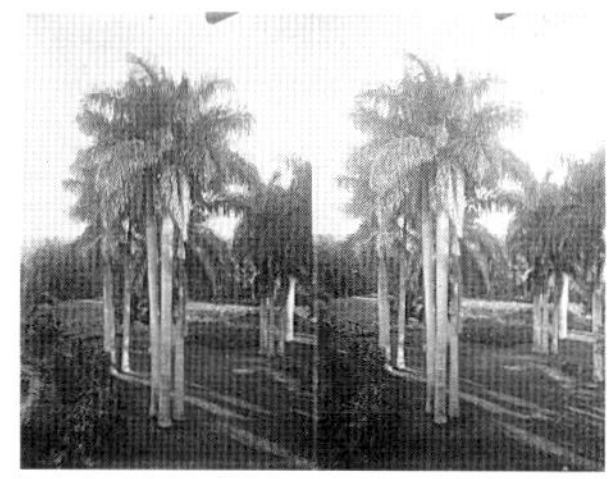

The royal palm (*Oreodoxa regia*) is more typical of Cuba than other islands and is particularly prolific in the island's eastern regions. In 1909, Johnston was struck by their abundance, noting that nearly every residence and farmstead was approached by avenues of royal palms. The same year, Jamaican writer H.G. DeLisser, following Johnston's route and style of documentation, remarked on *'the millions of slender, stately trees with their tapering whiteboles and towering crowns of green waving fronds'*. Returning in 1919 after the sugar boom, Delisser noted that the trees were being preserved.

B4460

7*

A Cuban Negro

Cuba

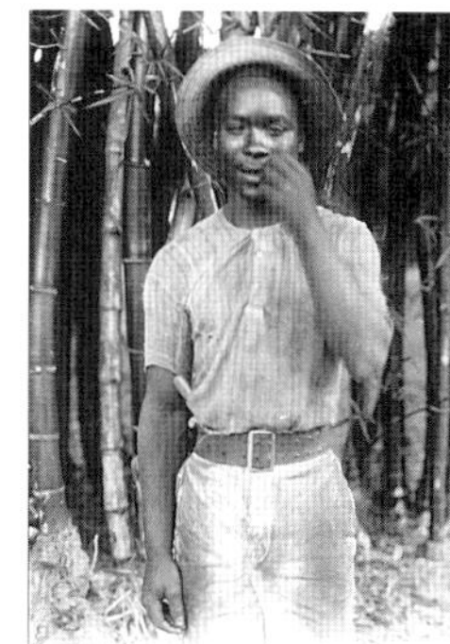

This black male plantation labourer is dressed in work garb *'after the fashion of Spanish peasants'*, according to Johnston. Casually smiling and chewing cane or tobacco, he poses boldly for the camera, in front of the *'cane piece'*. Although Johnston uses this image to represent a *'typical Cuban Negro'* and to reinforce distinctions between Negroes in the islands, the majority of blacks in cane producing parts of the island were not Cuban, but Jamaican and Haitian. The sudden expansion of Cuba's sugar industry had brought a wave of Caribbean immigrants, who, after emancipation, were free to take jobwork where economically viable. Jamaicans and Haitians flocked to the eastern province of Oriente, which is still predominantly black. Their purer African features suggest little, if any, Spanish blood.

B4462

8
Jamaican Negroes
Jamaica

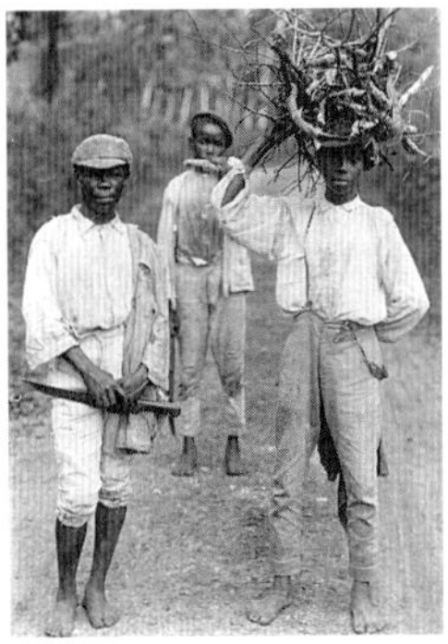

This image may have been taken while Johnston travelled through Portland, Jamaica's lushest parish. These teenage peasant boys are Maroons. Despite being barefooted, they are completely clothed, something Johnston considered a mark of civilisation.

B4464

9*
Maroon Negroes
Jamaica

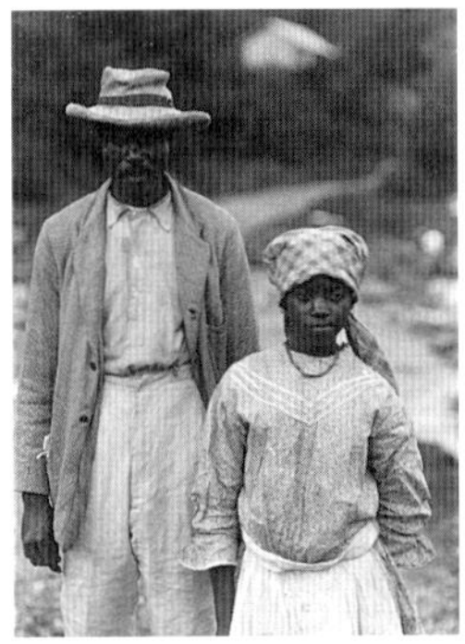

This portrait of father and daughter is taken outside Nanny Town, the Maroon village in eastern Jamaica. According to legend, Nanny was the leader of this community of runaway slaves in the 18th century. Also called Moore Town, it was one of four Maroon towns the British formally recognised in the treaty for the eastern Maroons signed by the Maroon leader Quao in 1740. The other towns were Accompong (St Elizabeth), Cudoe's Town (Trelawny) and Crawford Town (Portland). Johnston took several photographs in Nanny Town and detailed its rebellious history, impressed that these small communities withstood British rule.

B4466

10
Villages Near Blue Mountain
Jamaica

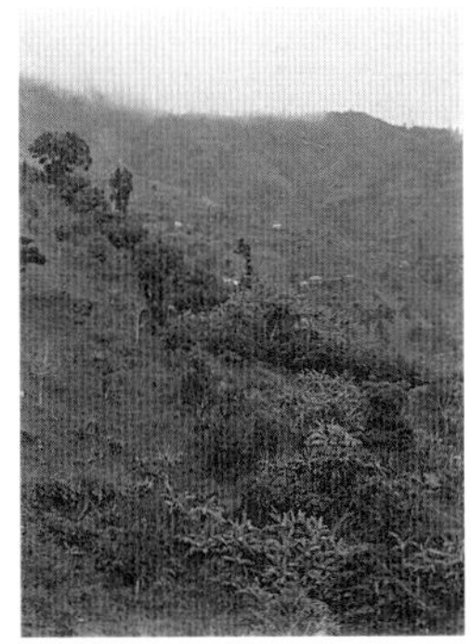

Crossing the Blue Mountains from Papine at the edge of Kingston, are Gordon Town and the Newcastle/Hardware Gap Road. Johnston used the latter, which was well plied and afforded a spectacular view as well as a resting place at the military camp in Newcastle. Several views *en route* might match this scene of the scrubby landscape with settlements in the distance. But the closest resemblance comes near Hardware Gap (highest point of the Blue Mountains) where a picturesque bend in the hillside opens up a scene of houses dotted amongst the green dense foliage.

B4467

11
A Negro Peasant returning from market
Jamaica

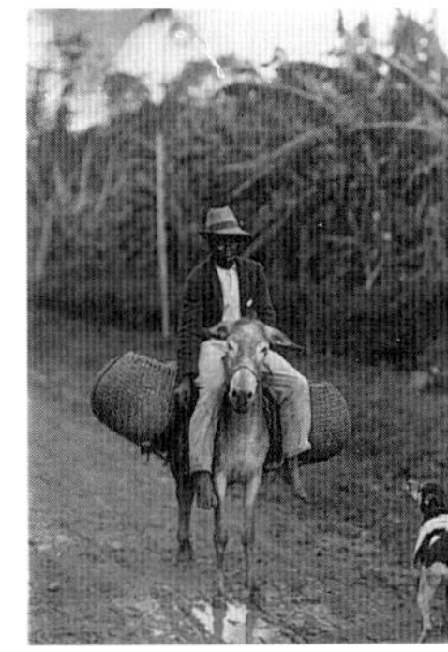

The man is riding a donkey burdened with hanging *bankra* through a 'banana walk' in eastern Jamaica. In *Jamaica the New Riviera: A Pictorial Description of the Island and its Attractions,* James Johnson records in 1907: *'There are many picturesque drives around Port Antonia, such as the Blue Hole six miles along the coast ... Moore town an old Maroon village, nine miles distant, romantically situated in a vale at the foot of Blue Mountains. This trip is full of interest passing on the way within view of the vast banana fields of Golden Vale'*. Harry Johnston followed a similar if not the same route where this picture was taken. He took other photographs of banana cultivation that he called *'the new wealth of Jamaica.'*

B4474

12
A Homestead
Haiti

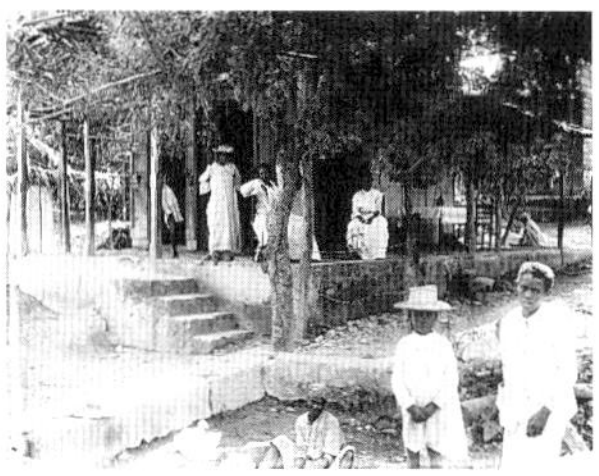

Johnston titled this domesticated scene of women and children, *A Haitian country house of the middle class type.* Those of status in the household are recognised by dress, with two of the women appearing to be servants. The wooden house is somewhat dilapidated but its generous veranda, concrete foundations, landscaped grounds suggest earlier wealth. Johnston described the houses in the suburbs of Port au Prince as: *'for the most part built by Germans and are really tasteful in architecture, cool, comfortable and surrounded by beautiful gardens.'*

c803

13
A River in Garmia(?)
Cuba

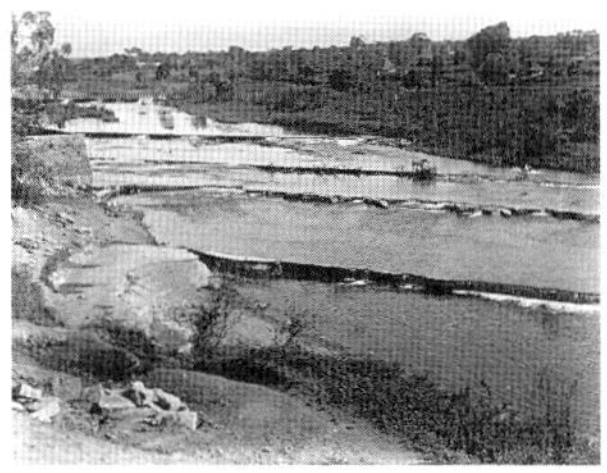

It is possible that this is the River Guama in the central province of Trinidad that Johnston encountered on his railway journey across the island to Havana. Johnston could have titled it according to its phonetic pronunciation. In his book he describes the Cuban rivers as being *'a succession of boiling rapids and snowy falls'* not unlike the scene captured here.

c804

14
Washing Clothes
Haiti

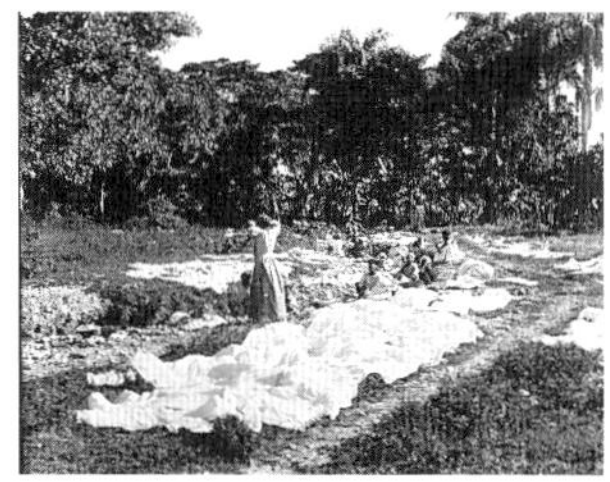

A river washing scene of this sort is typical of this era in Port au Prince. Less typically, both men and women are shown on the river bank surrounded by white sheets spread out over rocks. The consistency of the white sheeting and the royal palms in the background suggest that this may be a scene from an estate, possibly situated off the mountain road leading towards Boutilliers.

c806

15 *illustrated on back cover*
A Haitian Market
Haiti

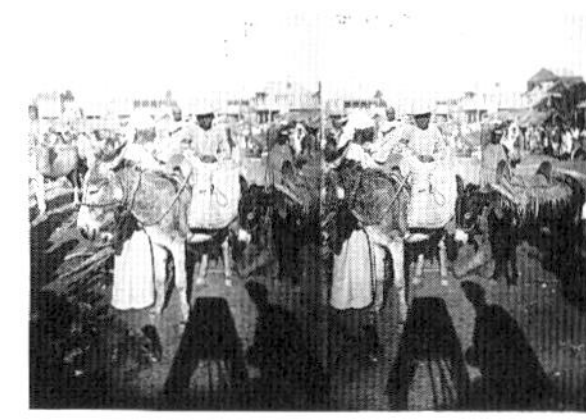

This is the only image where the photographer becomes participant. In the foreground, the camera and photographer's shadow intrude on the market scene. Other shadows indicate the public nature of this type of photography. Essentially a voyeuristic exercise, photography did not yet acknowledge the subjective eye in a period where it was used for ethnography, and where it was valued for its 'objectivity'.

c809

16
Coral on a Beach
Haiti

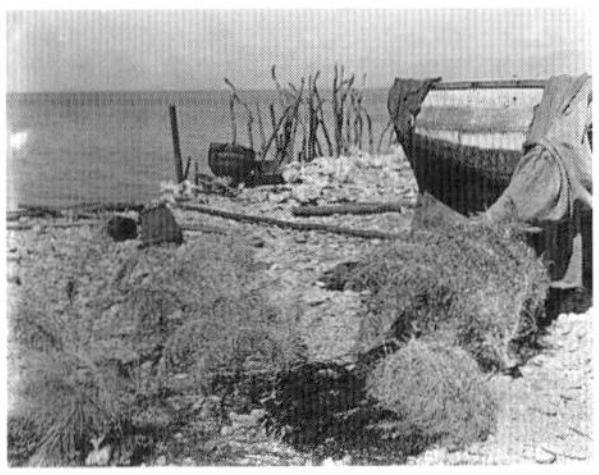

Because of his fascination with Caribbean marine life, Johnston gave these corals a fairly elaborate title and explanation. In *Negro in the New World* he called them *Crinoids fished up on the North Coast of Jamaica* and wrote: *'When first taken they are an exquisite mauve and pink, and though the full beauty of the colour fades enough remains for several years to make them into very decorative objects.'*

C812

17*
Burial Master, West Port au Prince
Haiti

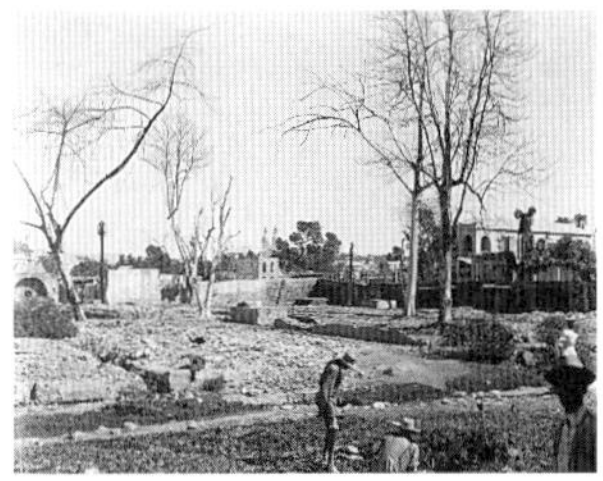

This glass plate labelled *Burial Master, West Port au Prince* refers to the man who appears to be over-seeing the digging in the foreground. But in *Negro in the New World* Johnston refers to this photograph as *'A portion of the town of Port au Prince burnt down by incendiary fires in August 1908'*. This fire, referred to as the *Morne a Tuf Incendie* of 5 July, was started by poorly stored military explosives that devastated that section of the city.

C814

18*
A Market Place, Port au Prince
Haiti

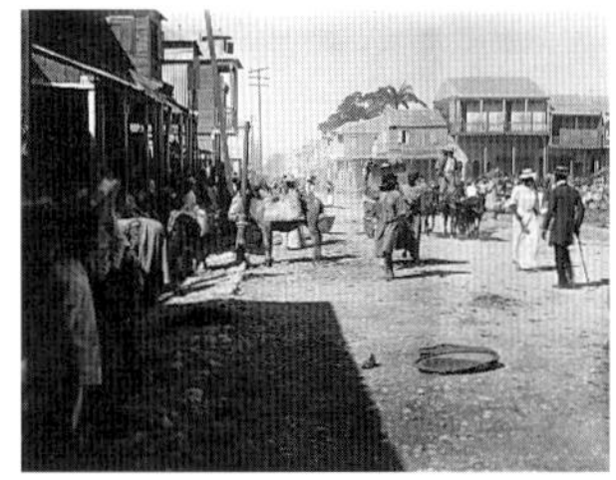

A section of the market in Port au Prince and commerce in the main street. Some middle class Haitians are depicted, distinctive by their refined clothing. But for the most part the scene is dominated by peasant traders and donkeys. The scene has a frontier quality about it: there is a sense of urgency in the movement of the people; the infrastructure seems unfinished and make-shift. Johnston described the streets during the dry weather as being dusty and intolerable with, *'no continuous sidewalk ... the paving is monstrous in its imperfections.'*

C810

19*
Cathedral, Port au Prince
Haiti

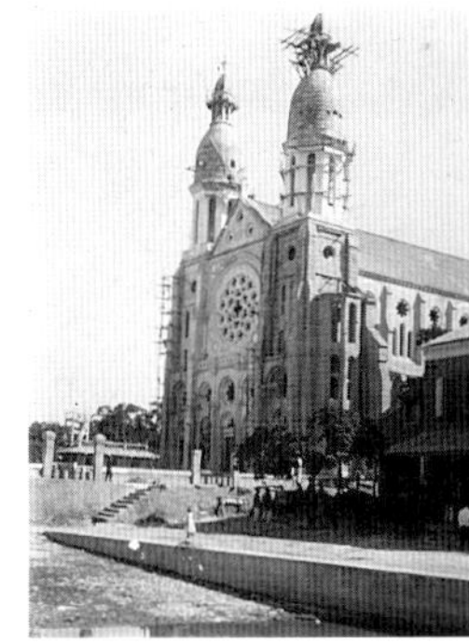

Of French design and Belgian construction, the unfinished Cathedral shows it has scaffolding. In other pictures its twin turrets dominate the cityscape. It is also distinctive for the expensive stained glass rosary window. Johnston noted its prominence when viewed from the sea and that it gave focus to the town. Despite strong feelings of anti-clericism by black nationalists, the Catholicism the French introduced played a more significant role in promoting scientific research and education in Haiti than other islands in the region.

C817

20*
Haitian Soldiers
Haiti

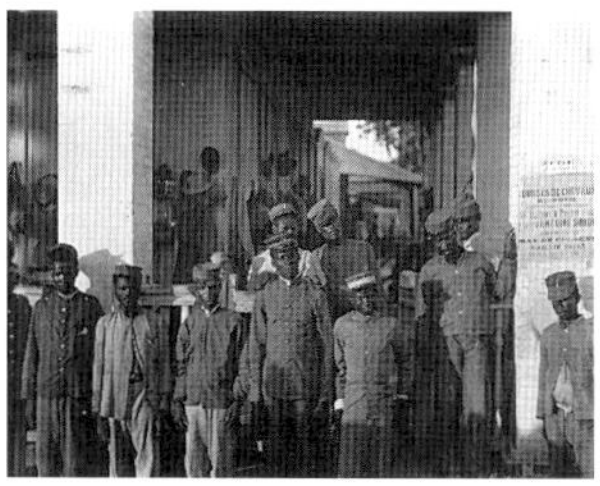

Harry Johnston arrived in Haiti just weeks after Antoine Simone's *coup d'etat* that ousted General Alexis on 2 December 1908. The men are dishevelled but fully attired in military dress. A few make an effort at attention while others seem more sceptical of the camera. These soldiers pose outside their barracks behind the President's Palace. Beside them, a poster announces the inauguration of the new President. Johnston makes no explicit statement about these soldiers, but given his mission to report to Theodore Roosevelt on the state of Haiti, this is both a significant as well as a poignant historical document.

c819

21
Lodge of the Stars, Masonic
Haiti

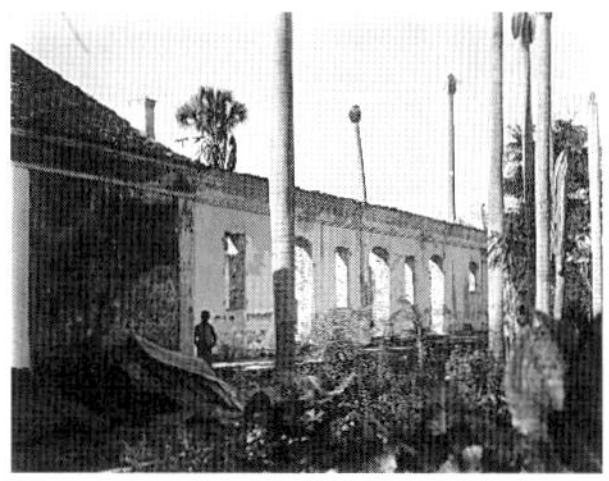

In the 18th century, the Freemasons played a major role in the cultural life of Haiti. The earliest masons were considered men of letters who maintained contact with France and progressive American masons such as Benjamin Franklin. Despite rivalry from Catholicism, every town had a lodge by 1840. This building housed *Etoile No 5*, the only Lodge of the Stars in Port Au Prince. Today, a newer lodge building is still run by *Les Pères Unis*.

c822

22
Haitian Women
Haiti

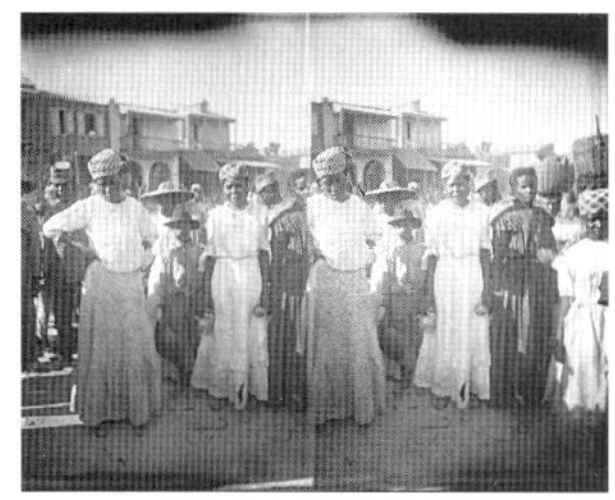

A group portrait of Haitian women taken near the market. Unlike their San Dominguan neighbours, Haitian women were the principal market vendors. This is a retention of African as opposed to Spanish traditions. In West Africa women also dominate market trading. Additionally, male attitudes in Haiti accommodated and even encouraged economic success for women.

c825

23
The President's Palace
Haiti

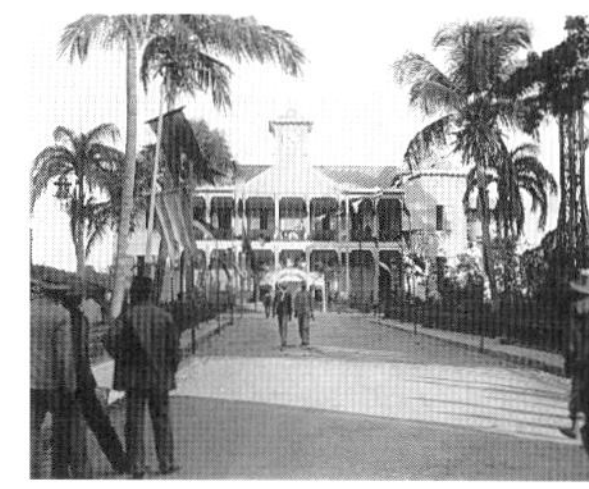

A rare image of the President's Palace before it was destroyed by explosives stored beneath it. Sitting at the end of a tree-lined avenue fronted by the extensive grounds of the Champ de Mars, the building, according to Johnston, is a *'turreted, verandahed erection, apparently roofed and faced with corrugated iron, or with some cold grey glistening metal'* with a general appearance that was not unpleasant, *'though a little baroque'*. He also tells us, however, that the grounds are ill-kept, dreary and trampled and *'perpetually paraded by soldiers.'* After the American invasion in 1915, the Palace was replaced by an American 'White House' as a symbol of democracy.

c828

24*
Lake Azuey, San Domingo
Dominican Republic

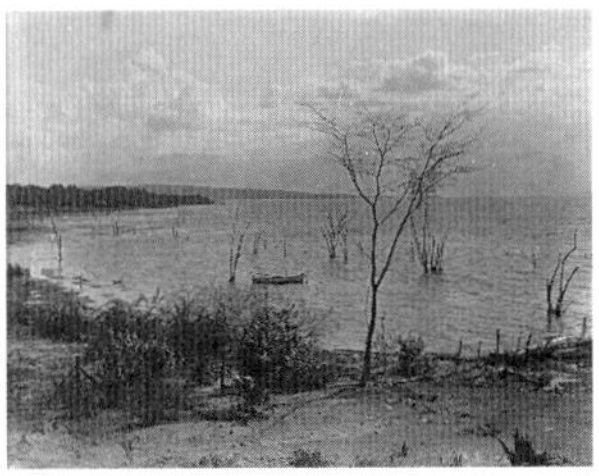

A large single glass plate negative, this landscape depicts the vast Lake Azuey, whose eastern banks border the Dominican Republic. It is a salt water lake surrounded by mountains, forests of *lignum vitae* and long stemmed pine trees. Johnston journeyed across the border into 'San Domingo', but did not study it as extensively as Haiti. Nevertheless, he made useful comparisons between the neighbouring countries because of their interrelated history and distinctly different cultures.

c829

25*
Haitian Woman with Children
Haiti

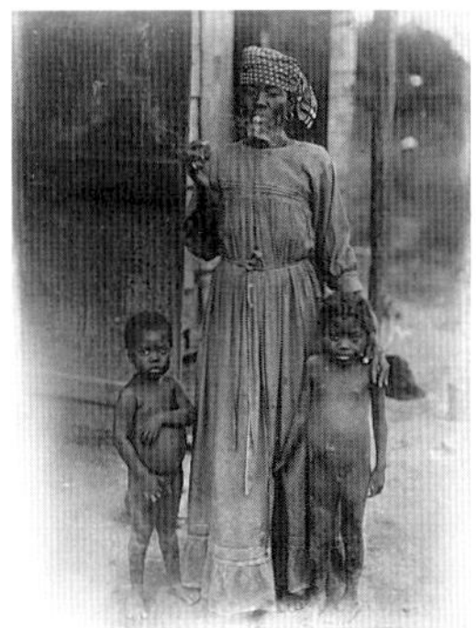

This Haitian woman with her children is antipathetic to Johnston's notions of civilisation, where dress, manner and attitudes to nudity are markers of refinement. This woman's stance, her confrontation with the camera, the way she defiantly breaks western taboos about female smoking and the protective gesture towards her children marks her as being more modern than civilised.

c831

26
The Government Secretariat and Offices, Port au Prince
Haiti

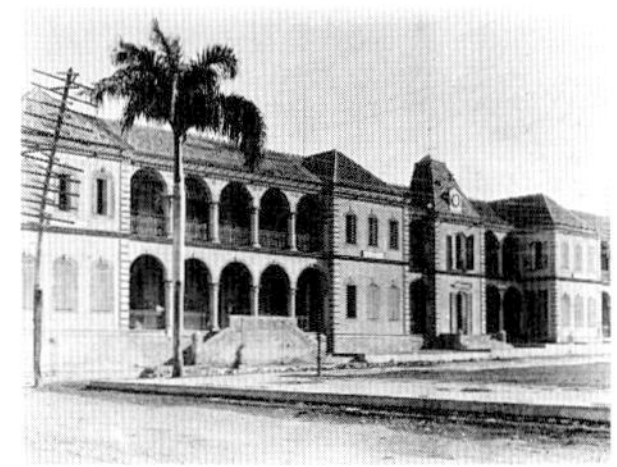

On the Champ de Mars, this is one of the few buildings to have had electricity and telephone service. Note the pole on the side of the building in Johnston's time. In the decade before his visit, this had been the seat of three military governments. Simon Sam (1896–1902). Nord Alexis (1902–08) and Antoine Simone (1908–11). These frequent shifts in power precipitated the United States' concerns for the island's political stability and its eventual occupation in 1915.

c832

27
Haitian Tombs
Haiti

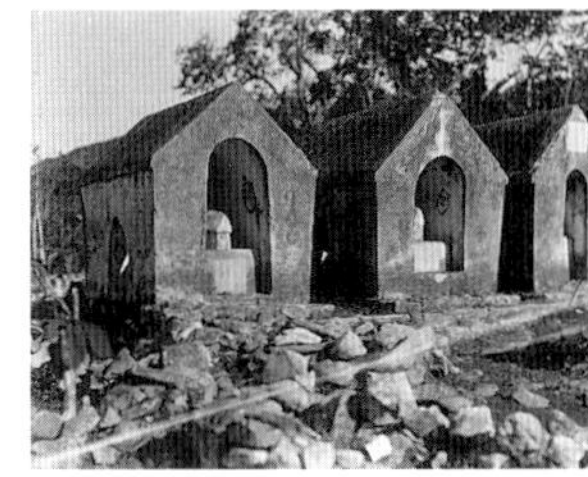

These tombs known as *Solomon Tombs* or *Vevette Solomon* were designed to incarcerate thousands who died as a result of a smallpox epidemic in 1902. The tombs are dotted throughout the countryside. Haitians say that the people of Port au Prince prayed to Our Lady of Perpetual Support and the epidemic immediately ceased.

c836

28*

An Agave: Lake Shore

Haiti

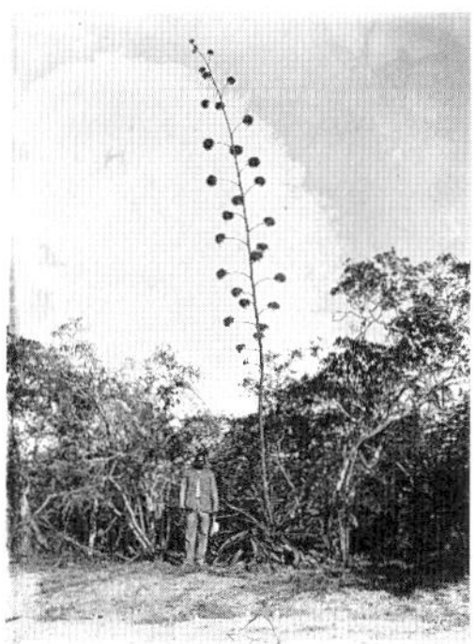

Characterised by its long stem, this cactus is called an *agave* and is found throughout the Caribbean. Its golden yellow flowers, surrounded by bright green lily leaves at its base, blossoms in the spring and is abundant on the dry hillsides of the region. The flower stalk can grow twenty to thirty feet tall. Johnston demonstrates the plant's unusual height by placing a man beside it. It is an unfortunate juxtaposition that brings to mind the taxonomic practices of the 18th and 19th centuries.

c841

29

A Cactus

Haiti

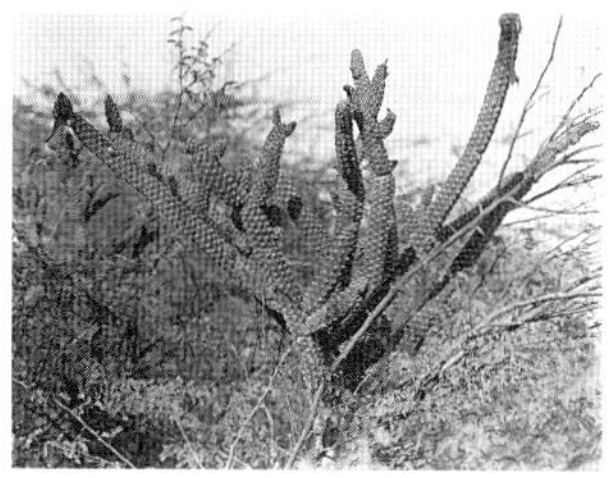

This *Pachycereus* cactus is a member of the *Cereus* family and is found in the Haitian lowlands. Arboreal cacti were of special interest to Johnston, who photographed each type. Of the *Pachycereus* he writes: *'A thornless type of cereus is so grotesque in the pointing of its fat, gouty fingers that it, together with another writhing snake-like arboreal cactus, might be fit surroundings of an enchanter's cave in a stage faerie.'* Johnston's description and the quality of his photography indicate that his interests in these plants was as much scientific as artistic.

c843

30

Tombs of the Political Martyrs

Haiti

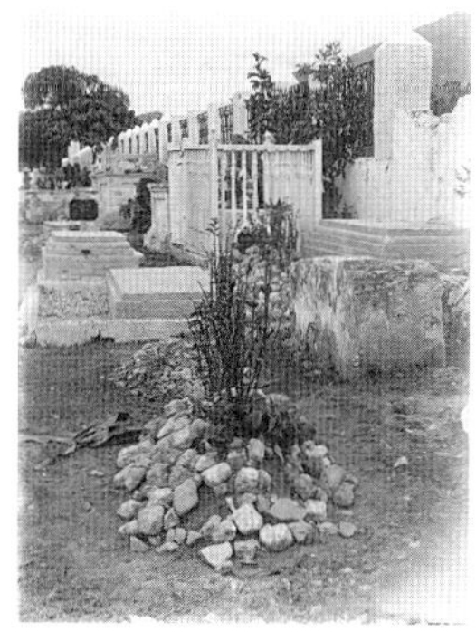

This is the innocuous looking site where executed mulatto objectors to General Alexis Nord's rule in the insurrections leading up to President Antoine's *coup d'etat* were buried. The coup took place in December 1908 just weeks before Johnston's arrival. In *Negro in the New World* Johnston titles this work as *Outside the Cemetery, Port au Prince*. The disparity between the two titles may be significant, suggesting that Johnston may have wished to play down the political aspect of this image for the sake of the publication.

c845

31

Precipitous Mountain Side

Jamaica

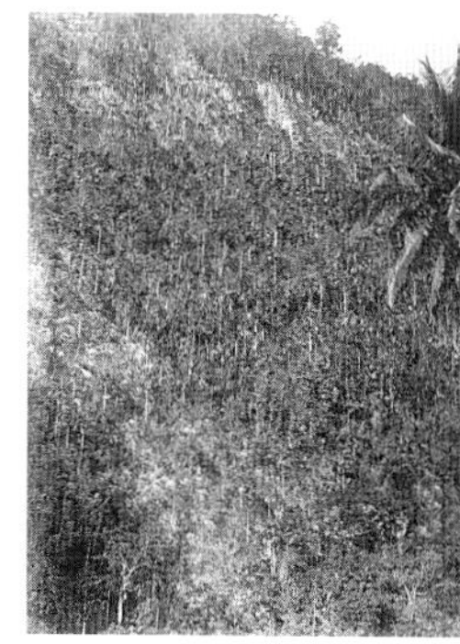

The precipitation on this cliffside on the banks of the Rio Cobra in Bog Walk Gorge aroused Johnston's botanical interest. He travelled through the gorge, then a popular attraction, either on buggy from nearby Ewarton, or by the train that ran between Spanish Town and Ewarton, or in a canoe along the river starting at Bog Walk Village. In *Through Jamaica with a Kodak*, the author, A. Leader, describes Bog Walk as a photographer's paradise. *'Almost immediately on leaving the little village'*, he writes *'the river enters a magnificent gorge, its passive fern decked rock wall rising on the right, almost perpendicularly about nine hundred feet'*.

c847

32
Spanish Town
Jamaica

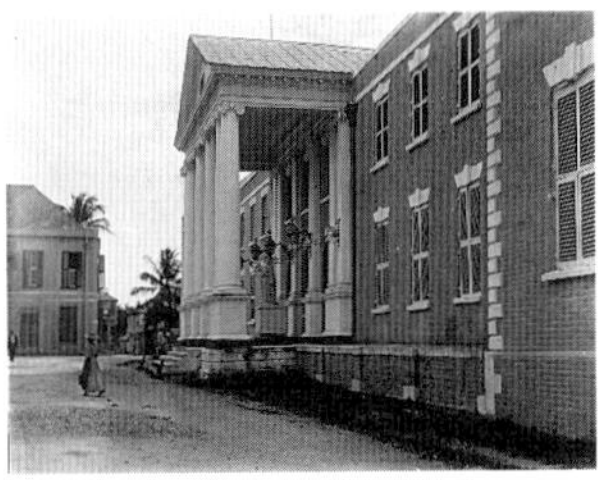

Johnston calls these Georgian buildings in Spanish Town Square *'stately'. 'Around the Plaza or square, you will see about everything of interest there is in the place.'* writes James Johnston in *Jamaica the New Riviera* (1907).

'On one side stands the Old King's House, or official residence of the Governors when Spanish Town was the capital. With its massive porticoes supported by Doric columns, inside you will find the entrance hall, banqueting hall, ballroom and reception rooms all on a scale so grand and lofty that one feels like being turned loose in a cathedral of huge dimensions. Then repair to the Rio Cobre Hotel for lunch and on to a drive through the Bog Walk ...'

Harry Johnston likely visited Spanish Town, using the hotel Rio Cobra as a base. Founded by the Spaniards in 1523, Spanish Town was first called St Jago de la Vega and became the capital of Jamaica after the Port Royal earthquake in 1692.

C849

33*
A Country School
Jamaica

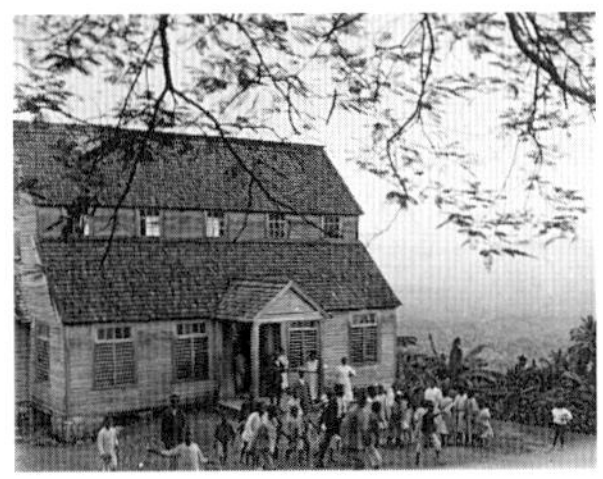

This large two-storey school in central Jamaica no longer exists, but it could have been the old Barracks Junior School in Claremont, St Ann. Primary schools of this type were normally run by Christian organisations, since comprehensive state education was not available immediately after emancipation.

C850

34*
Haitian Mountains
Haiti

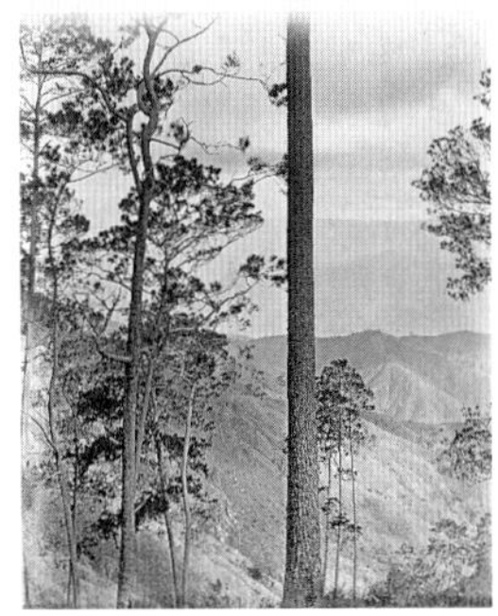

In the mountains near Kenscoff above Port Au Prince, looking towards Obleon, the view today remains the same except for the scarring of the hillside from deforestation.

C855A

35 *illustrated on front cover*
A Jamaican Negro
Jamaica

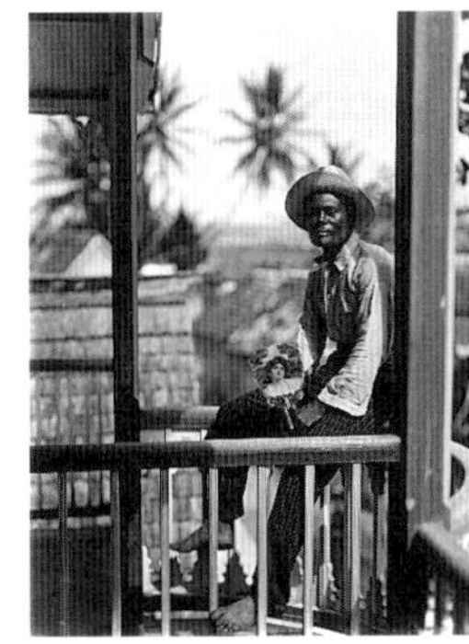

Johnston calls this portrait of a barefooted black man, astride the balustrade of balcony *A Jamaican Artisan*. He holds a fan that the title suggests he made. Very little documentation exists that provides evidence of black artistry or craftsmanship for this period. This has led many historians to conclude that black creativity as witnessed in Africa had been stymied by the colonial experience. Photographs such as this prove otherwise. The fan is decorated with the portrait of a white woman. This juxtaposition of black man to white female image and all its connotations of prejudice, self-hate, and self-perception, make this an ironic, informative and powerful image.

C855B

36
The Splendid Mountains of Haiti ...
Haiti

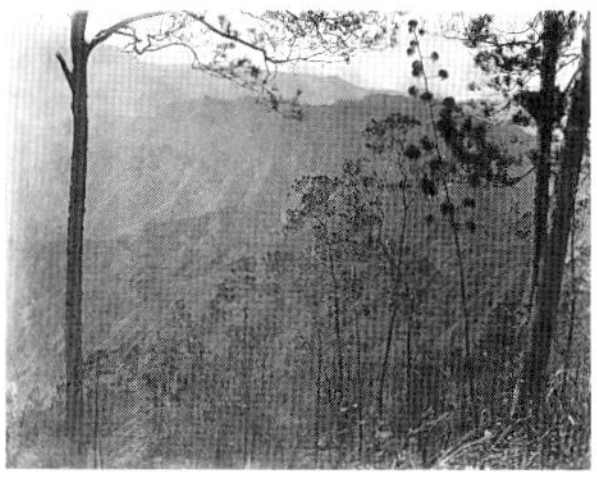

Johnston's full title – *'The Splendid Mountains of Haiti ... wherein the French Soldiers found the Haitian Negroes unconquerable'* – alludes to general Toussaint Louverture's bid for independence in 1801 when Napoleon's military tried to force the 'wayward' colony of Saint Domingue into submission. With his army of former slaves, Louverture waged guerrilla war from these familiar mountains. Their military strikes and a yellow fever epidemic wiped out thousands of Napoleon's imperial army and halted his ambitions for the country that became the world's first black republic in 1804.

C846

37*
A Jamaican Farmer or Beekeeper
Jamaica

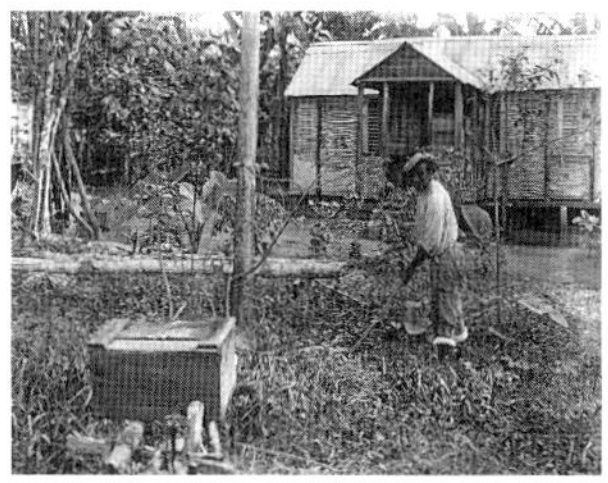

The ideal of most of the peasantry after emancipation was land ownership and economic independence. This industrious small farmer / beekeeper hoeing land in front of his wattle and daub home is typical of the period. The ground provisions visible are dasheen and cassava. In the background are fruit trees and in the foreground his bee-box for producing honey. This kind of cultivation ensured self sufficiency for the black peasantry, supplying produce for family needs with any extra being sold at the market. By 1900, many farmers in the region were also able to expand their production to include cash crops such as sugar, coffee, rum, pimento and ginger for export and greater profits.

C858B

38
Haitian Mountains
Haiti

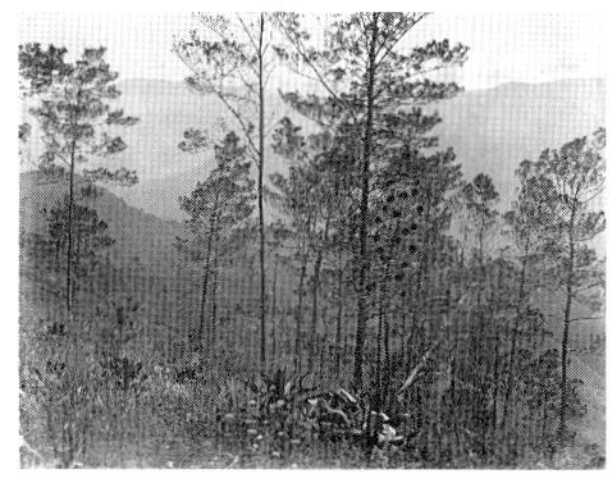

Of scenes such as this Johnston wrote *'In the dells of the mountains, about 4000 feet, are handsome jungles of tree ferns. Everywhere the glossy green agave, with its column of gold flower clusters. The aromatic scent of the pine woods is indescribably good to the jaded white man exhausted with the tropics'.*

C861A

39*
Entrance of a Vudu Shrine
Haiti

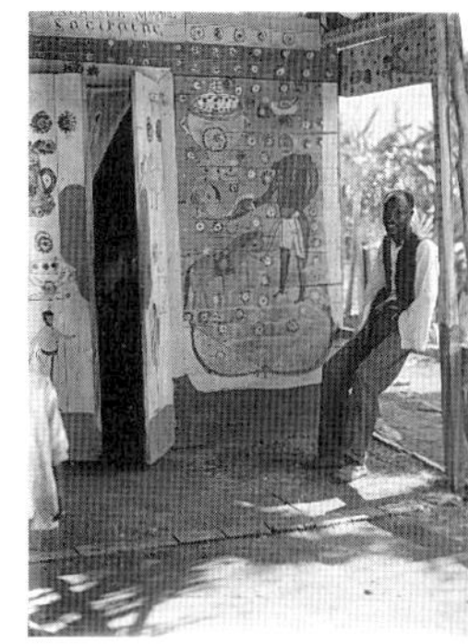

Voodoo beliefs are based on West African spiritualism. When the Haitian colonial authorities banned slaves from practising their rituals, they camouflaged their worship with aspects of Catholicism and freemasonry. This syncretism is evident in the mysterious signs and symbols used to decorate this voodoo shrine or *Houmfort* which is a mix of African and European imagery. Voodoo's cosmology of symbols and the secrecy surrounding certain of its practices led many Europeans to exaggerate and condemn its practice as cannibalistic, devil worship, and Johnston challenged and dismissed these allegations.

C867A

40
Vudu Drums
Haiti

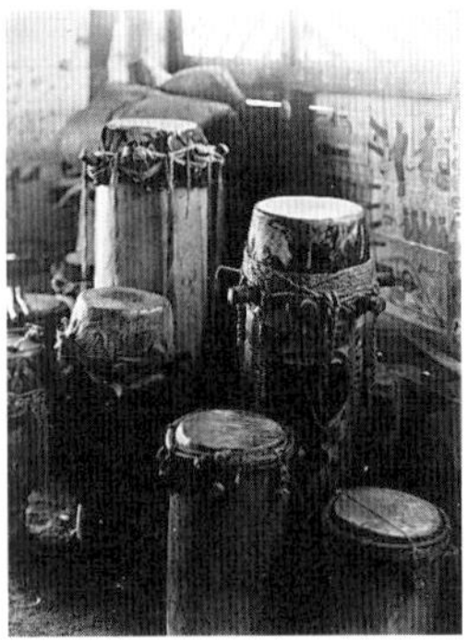

This photograph taken inside the shrine also depicted in this exhibition (cat. 39), has similar imagery on the walls. The drums are ceremonial, played during voodoo rituals. There are three sizes *Maman, Papa* and *Boula* or *Cata* (baby). They are long and cylindrical and made from a single hollowed out tree trunk. The tops with cowhide or goat skin, tied in place with cord wound around pegs on the side of the drum. These drums are also painted although it is difficult to make out the design. Usually, they have symbolic markings, such as snakes, to represent the god Damballa, or a heart shape for Ezili, the Virgin Mary. The drums are played during the voodoo ceremony to invoke Gods of the *Lwa* or the spiritual realm.

C868A

41
A View of Port au Prince
Haiti

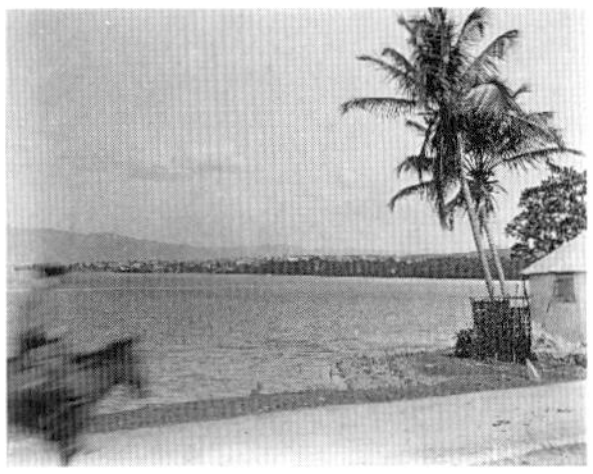

A view of the coast road to Leogane looking across the harbour towards Port au Prince. The city stretches out horizontally in the distance. Johnston described this scene as he approached Port au Prince by ship: *'The open arms of Haiti are two peninsulas of alpine heights that enclose a vast gulf of sheltered sea screened from rough winds and vexing currents: a gulf which would make the safest and amplest naval station in the world.'* It is an ironic description given Johnston's mission to investigate the state of Haiti for Theodore Roosevelt, the United States gunboat patrolling off the coast and their eventual occupation of Haiti in 1915.

C869A

42
Woman Offering Author an Orchid
Jamaica

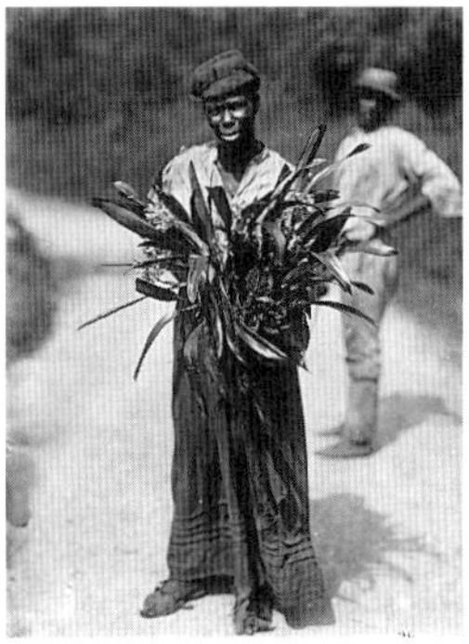

The orchid shown here could be the *Broughtania Sanguinia* which flowers in many colours, and perhaps is the most common variety in Jamaica today. The Caribbean has several rare orchid varieties, many of which were taken to Europe in the colonial period. *Encyclia Cochleata* and *Encyclia Fragrens* were the first Jamaican species to bloom in Europe (Kew Gardens) in 1787 and 1788.

C869B

43
Moneague
Jamaica

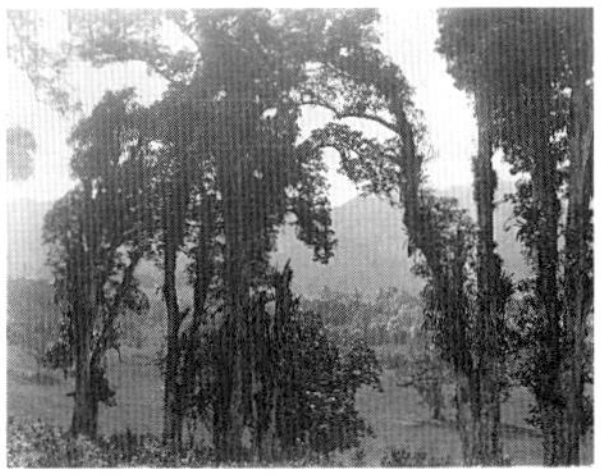

The unusually formed trees in the foreground against the backdrop of pasture land and mountains could almost be mistaken for a scene in Europe, and is probably the reason Johnston described it as parkland. Johnston's title for this photograph is *The district of Moneague in the central parklands of Jamaica, 2000 ft above sea level.* Although Johnston does not mention it, he may have stayed at the Moneague Hotel, built by the government in anticipation of Jamaica's Great Exhibition of 1891 and recently refurbished to attract tourists. The hotel was on a well plied route leading to Fern Gully and Ocho Rios, a comfortable and picturesque trip for Johnston.

C870B

44

Sacred Trees and Offerings, Vudu Writings

Haiti

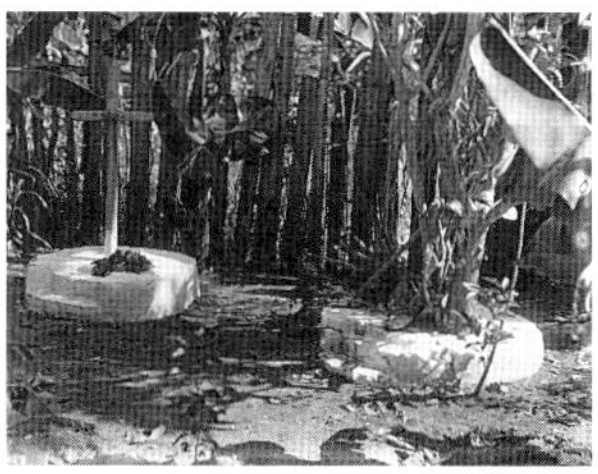

These funerary crosses and stones (*Lakou*) mark the spot where spirits are buried. Offerings are placed beneath the crosses as gifts. They are diverse, bundled and bottled, containing rum, candles, herbal medicines, fruit, vegetables, foodstuffs, luck stones, bones, wools, minerals etc., dependant upon the demands of the spirits (*Lwa*).

C871

45*

A Market of Fish, Port au Prince

Haiti

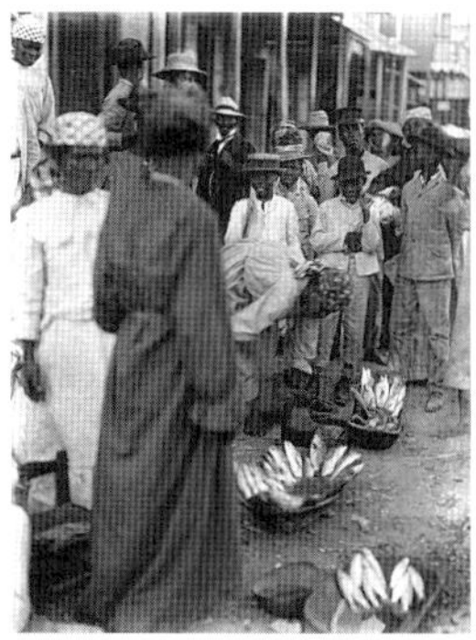

One of the few photographs Johnston took that appears orchestrated. The crowd seems curious about something. Perhaps Johnston, who later writes more about the fish than the people, may have been setting up the fish to photograph. *'Some of the women in the market-place are selling fish which an artist would purchase for their colours alone. They look like the* poissons d'Avril *in Eastertide shop-windows ... such combinations of blue and orange, scarlet and mauve, yellow and black, pink and green.'*

C872A

46

A Negro Store, Ewarton

Jamaica

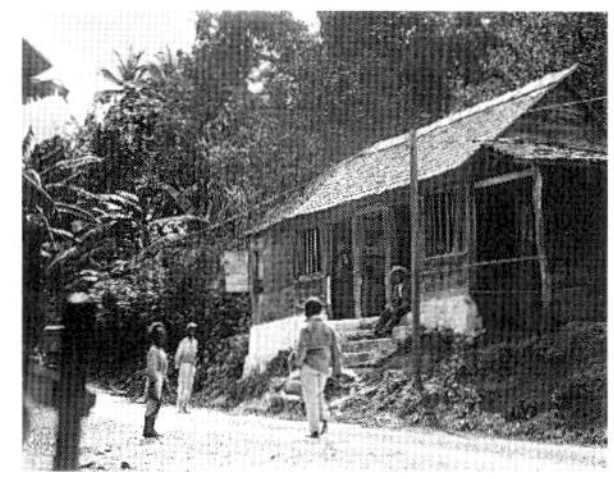

Constructed from wood on a stone base with steps at the doorway, this shop is now a bar and betting shop and still stands on the main road in Ewarton, one of Jamaica's bauxite towns. Run by a 68-year-old lady who bought it from the Fong family in 1967, she remembers the shop was one of few in the village. Apart from electricity and the shingled roof covered with corrugated iron, little has changed.

C876

47* *frontispiece*

Negro Peasant Woman

Jamaica

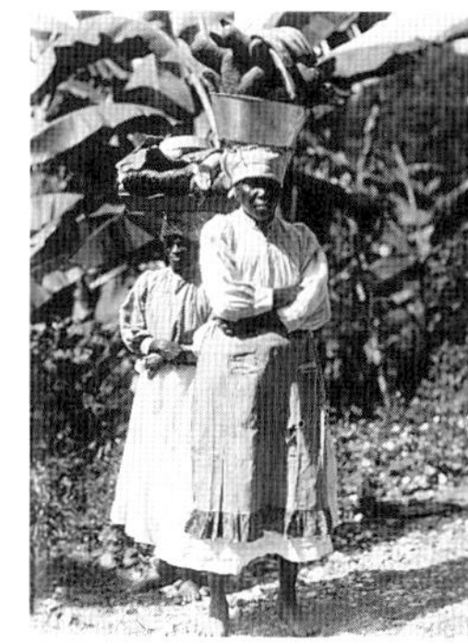

Johnston saw this young female resolutely with arms akimbo in a 'banana walk' in Jamaica as the archetypal 'primitive' living in harmony with nature. Writing about such women he quotes at length Ralph Hall Caine's, *The Cruise of Port Kingston*: *'... nowhere in the whole of the world can she be excelled in beauty of form and grace of carriage ... Her neck is neither long nor short, nor fat, nor lean, but shoulders, neck and chest are all revelations of the woman who is leading a life close to primitive nature ...'* The image is typical of 19th century ethnographic photography that sought to ennoble, authenticate and document, non-western civilisations.

C930

48*
Cuban Negroes at Play
Cuba

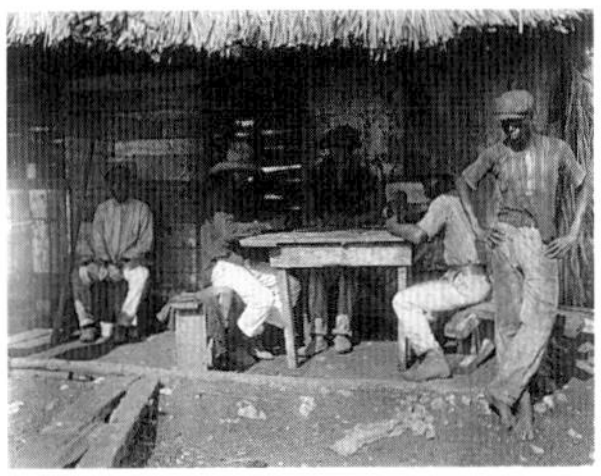

Johnston titles this image *Cuban Negroes playing dominoes during their midday rest*. Perhaps not all these men are Cuban. Many were probably Jamaicans and Haitians working with Cubans in the cane field of Oriente. An 18th century Italian game, dominoes was originally introduced to the Caribbean by the Spanish.

c881

49*
Negroes at Work
Cuba

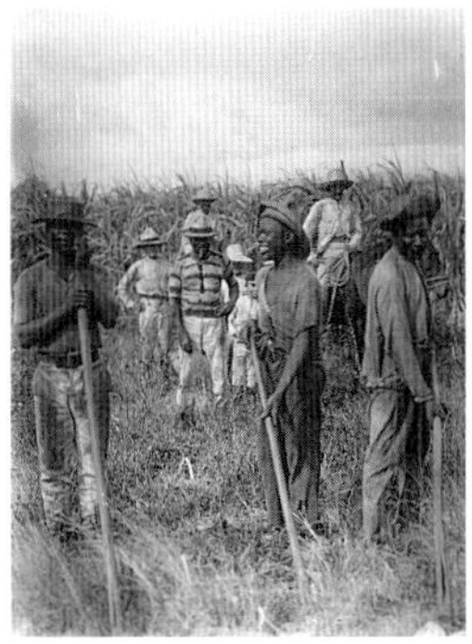

Taken on a sugar estate in Oriente, eastern Cuba, this image is of cane workers supervised by horsemen dressed in Spanish style who wear 'Panama' hats. These foremen on the plantation were called *Capatoz* in Cuba, and *Bushers* in Jamaica. Both labourers and supervisors seem aware of the camera. Johnston inexplicably does not give this group a specific nationality, as he does for other photographs.

c883

50
Cuban Wagoners (Negroes)
Cuba

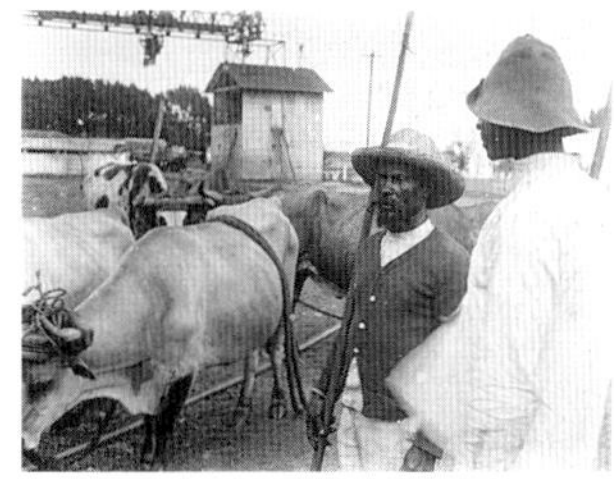

This photograph was taken on a property that Johnston visited in eastern Cuba. The use of oxen suggest that it was not then mechanised. When Johnston visited, Cuba was on the verge of a sugar boom that would transform its economy. Making his second visit in twenty years to Cuba in 1929, H.G. de Lisser recounts: '*... as far as the eye can reach, one sees cane and yet more cane, a vast carpet of it, light green and rolling away from side to side across whole breadth of Cuba.*' Johnston's depiction of the cane fields is similar to his depiction of bananas in Jamaica, illustrating his concern for the development of agricultural economies in the Caribbean.

c884

51
Cane Peddlers
Cuba

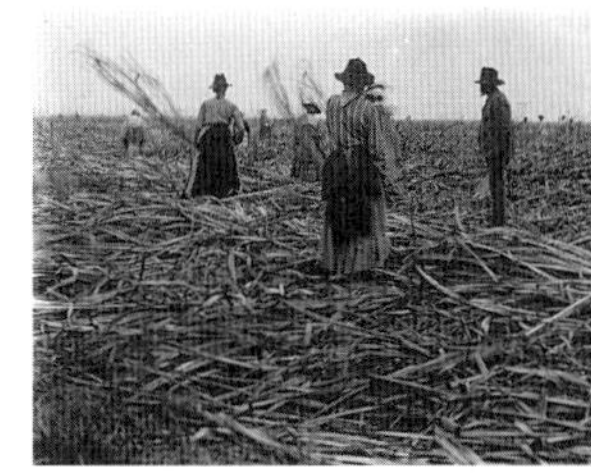

In the 19th century slavery's abolition and competition from sources closer to European markets seriously undermined sugar's viability in the Caribbean. After emancipation, economically motivated men and women wayfared the islands negotiating different cultures and languages to earn a living. Regularly plying Caribbean waters with tourists and produce, steamboats linked the islands and opened up the Americas. The peddlers pictured here are typical of labour gangs working on estates by the day or by the task, and represented a new kind of labour force. The scene also shows that women were not exempted from agricultural labour.

c887

52
Maroons
Jamaica

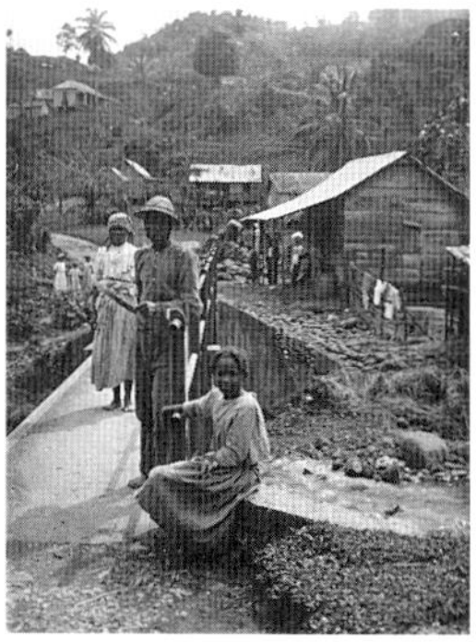

New Nanny town in Portland was to become one of four permanent sites for runaway slaves, known as Maroons or *Cimarrones* (sp. mountaineers) since the 17th century. This photograph is taken by the bridge that spans the river at the entrance to the Maroon town. The bridge acts as a natural barrier for the community. Situated high in the Portland hills, the town has a broad panoramic view that made it secure for this community of runaway slaves. The hills also contained paths leading to more densely forested areas that could provide escape routes into the John Crow mountains.

c895

53*
In the Maroon Country
Jamaica

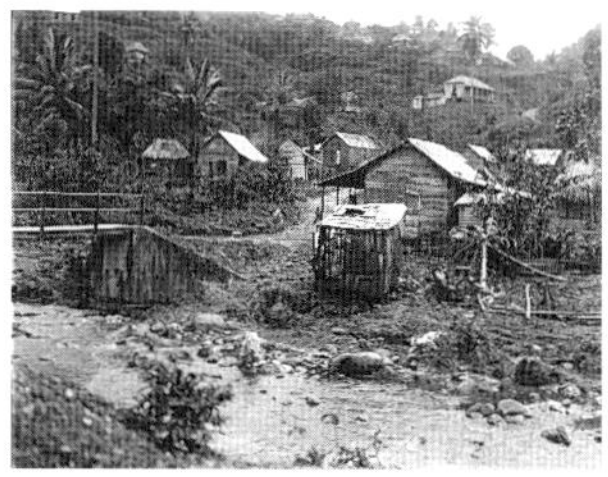

The most significant figure in this picture is the person washing in the river. A garment obscures the face, forcing us to wonder whether it is a shield from the sun or from the camera's intrusion. Although he praised the hospitality of Jamaicans, Johnston believed that the Maroons were the single exception. He wrote that during this visit to the Maroons of north eastern Jamaica he found them *'insolent and disobliging, and inclined to levy blackmail on anyone who passed through their villages and plantations and wished to photograph the scenery.'*

c892

54*
In Port Maria
Jamaica

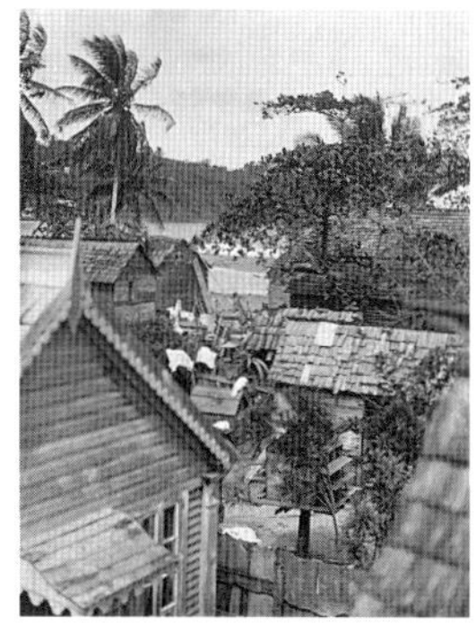

Taken in the hills of Port Maria overlooking the bay and the backs of houses in the town showing washing hung out to dry, this photograph is a very potent and intimate image. Johnston records that: *'Personally, I found that without exception all classes and all colours in Jamaica are exceptionally civil and obliging to the stranger: even the stranger like myself who was (with the best of intentions) prying into back yards, photographing many things and many human types, and often in too much of a hurry to request permission or explain the motive.'*

c898

55
House of Assembly
Barbados

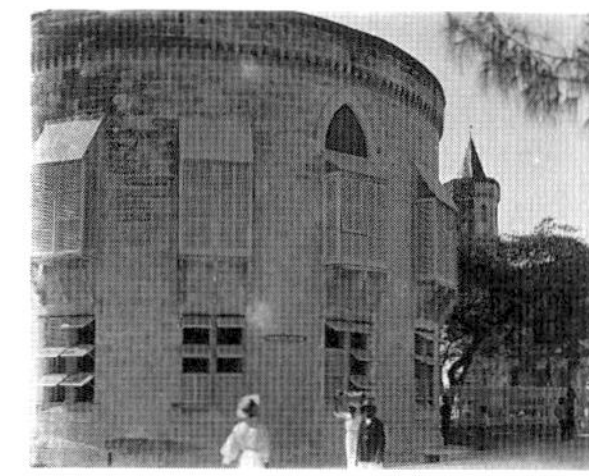

One of the oldest Houses of Assembly in the world, this Barbadian institution in Palmeto Square dates back to the 17th century. The circular, brick building with shuttered windows on both floors has changed little except for an additional wing that obscures the view that Johnston documented. The House of Assembly faces the waterfront, but this picture was taken at the rear of the building from the busy market square directly behind.

c899

56
In The Market, Bridgetown
Barbados

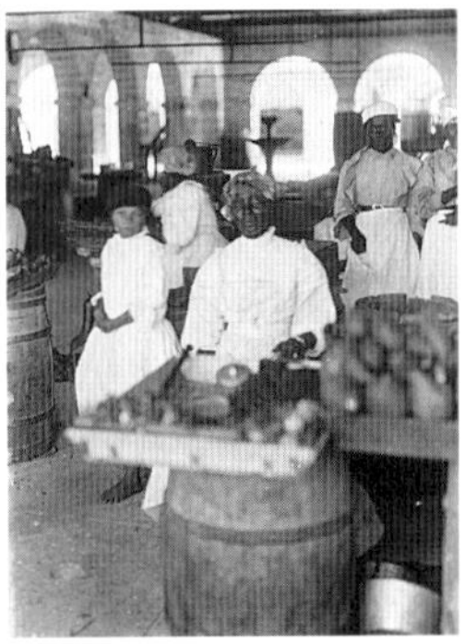

Inside Bridgetown's main market, peasants sold crops left from the family's subsistence farming. Recent studies of post-emancipation years show that Caribbean women's market trading was a carry over from West African tradition that gave them an economic independence different from their European counterparts.

C900

57*
A Road Outwards, the Country
Barbados

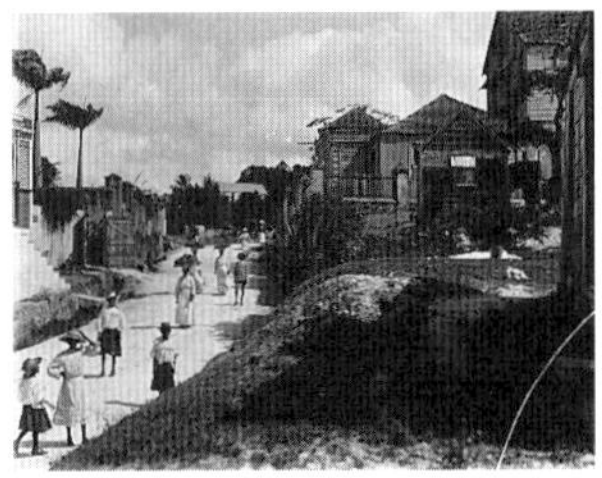

This may be the main road out of Bridgetown leading up to Eagle Hill and Spike's Town. It is difficult to be exact since most of the main roads running out of the capital are carved from rocks and feature similar raised banks. The width of the road and imposing residential homes fronted by walls, fences and gates suggest urban wealth close to the town centre.

C902

58
Barbados
Barbados

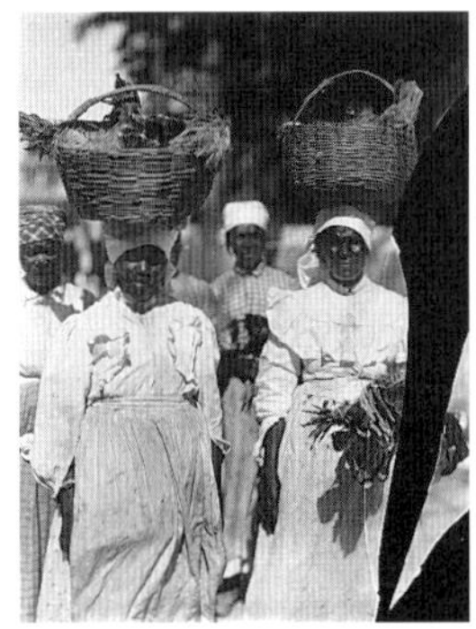

These women are carrying poultry to the market for sale, posing characteristically with their loads balanced on their heads. In contrast to Haiti's vendors, their produce is dead rather than live. After emancipation, the peasantry got only small parcels of land, limiting them to kitchen garden cultivation. They sold chickens, pigs and goats to diversify their market trade.

C903

59
Busy Barbados
Barbados

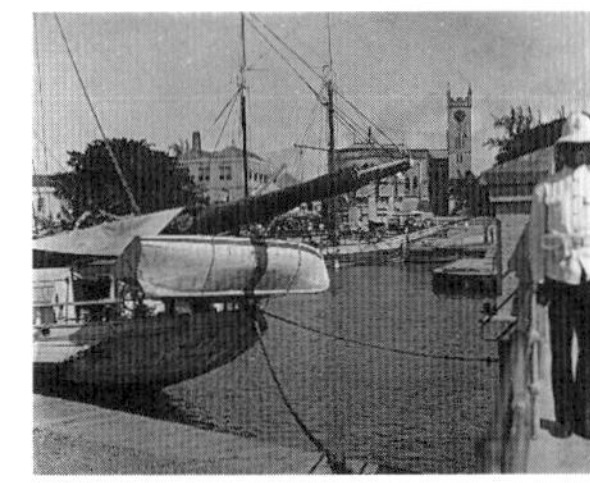

Johnston represented the Caribbean as a place of law and order. He keenly documented all aspects of its development and westernisation. Whenever possible he includes policemen as a sign of refinement. This scene also captures the hustle and bustle of the town and the prominent buildings such as the House of Assembly and its clocktower from the other side of the quay.

C904

60

St Mary's Church

Barbados

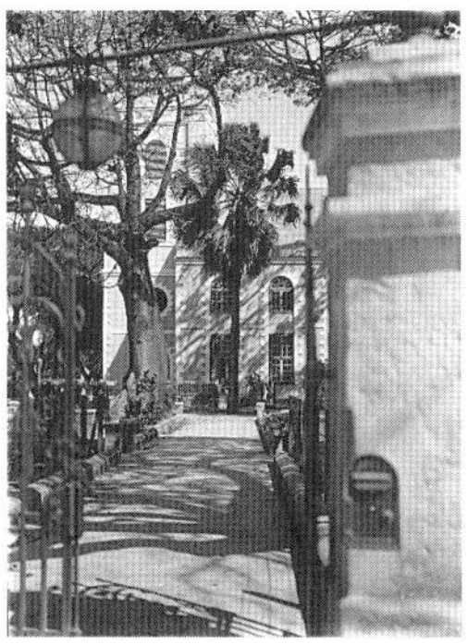

St Mary's Church in Barbados was erected in the 17th century. It is brick and the facade is decorated in regency design. An electric lamp is strung over the top of the gateway of the church, which is a brief walk from the House of Assembly at the end of Bridge Street. Johnston would have passed St Mary's on his way in to the countryside.

c1905

61

The Port of Bridgetown, Barbados

Barbados

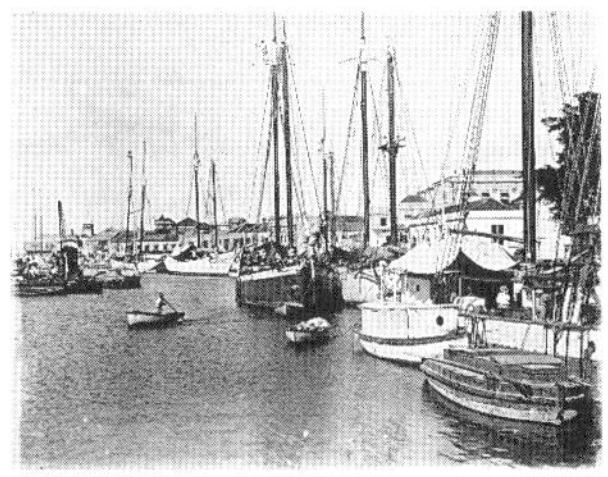

The town of Bridgetown with all its brick buildings is clearly visible beyond the port. This photograph appears to have been taken from the second bridge looking down the *careenage* (inner harbour) as the water flows out to the sea. During the 18th century, the port became a haven for Britain's naval and military forces in the wars with France and Spain. By the time of Johnston's arrival in 1909 it is seen as more picturesque than functional. '*... blue green water, white schooners, with chains painted like necklaces of coral,*' he writes.

c1907

62*

Negro Pottery

Barbados

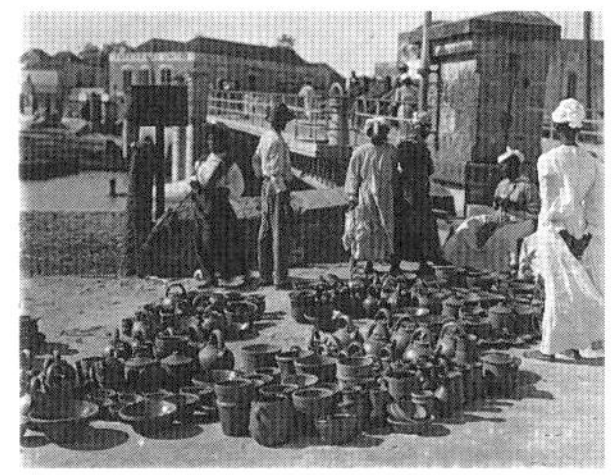

The clay pots or *Yabbas*, (dialect of the *Twi* word *Ayawa*, which means earthen vessel or dish) for sale here were essentially functional. *Yabbas* ranged in size from small shallow bowls to large heavy deep ones and were used for cooking. The array of clay items shows a facility for pot-making inherited from West African tradition, a creative endeavour that was retained during slavery. This photograph is a rare document of artistic / creative production during this period. Johnston believed there was something indigenous and original about Caribbean craft that was not reflected in what he considered the facile arts and crafts movement in England. About the use of colour and design he wrote '*... I shall not live to see it ... but I am sure that the Negro Race some day, ... is going to astonish the world in the arts of Design and Music.*'

c1908

63

Bromeliacaceous Epiphile

Jamaica

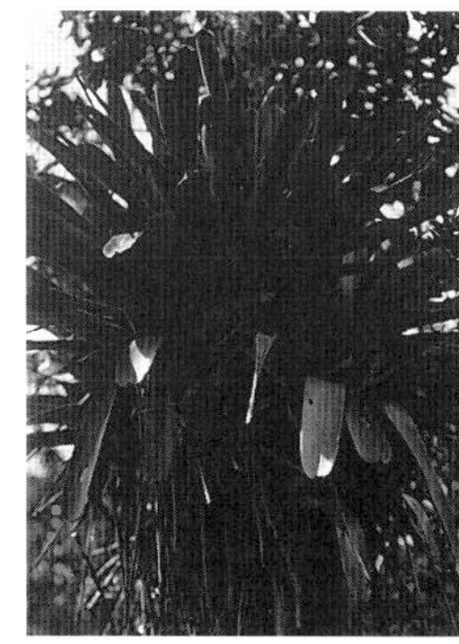

The *Bromeliacaceous Epiphile (Hobenbergia)* is a parasitic plant regularly found attached to the silk cotton trees that support other plant forms such as aroids, ferns, cacti and orchids. In Jamaica, Bromeliaceae's are called 'wild pine' because of their resemblance to pineapple plants. This photograph focuses on a single multi leafed plant. The 'nests' hang abundantly from trees lining the route over Mount Diablo and are particularly prolific around Moneague, St Ann.

c1914

64
Eojuinie Columnia?
Jamaica

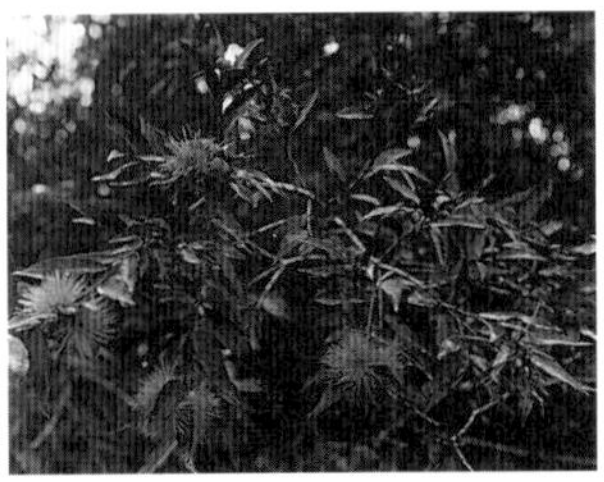

Johnston's handwriting makes it difficult to identify this accurately. The *columnia* genera are noted for their multicellular hairy blossoms/or fruit normally of yellow, red, pink colour. It is possible that Johnston considered this plant a new species or that he identified this shrub as being a cross between the *Eugenia* and *Columnia* genera.

C916

65
Gllirridicia
Jamaica

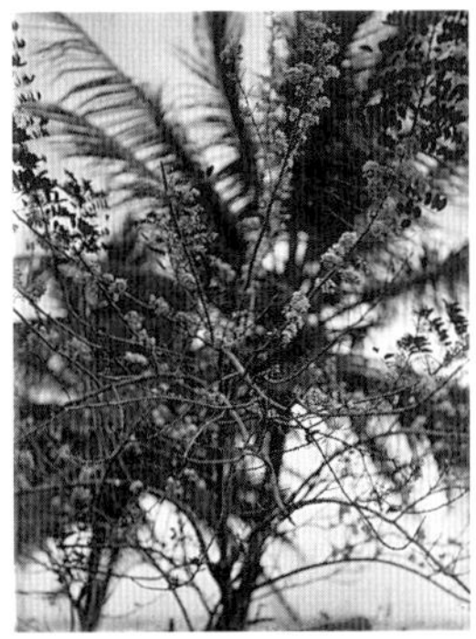

The *Gllirridicia* or 'rat catcher' is a winter blooming tree. Between January and March its lavender-pink bean blossoms resemble Japanese sprays.

C917

66*
Street in Port Maria/Road in Jamaica
Jamaica

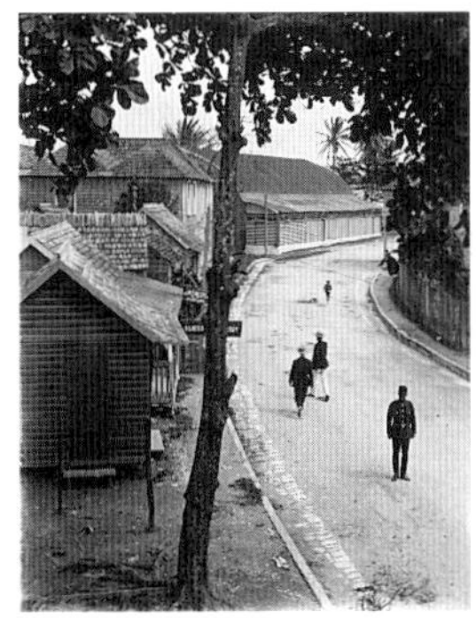

Johnston tells us that this photograph represents: *'Sunday in a small Jamaican country town'* (Note the policeman, who the author found subsequently to be, a most intelligent, civil spoken guide). The modern signage identifies this street as Port Maria's main commercial strip. Port Maria's centre has changed dramatically since 1908, with the market square and shopping areas moving a few blocks, and the picturesque bridge that served the main road now derelict.

C923

67
The Shallow Coasts of Western Trinidad
Trinidad

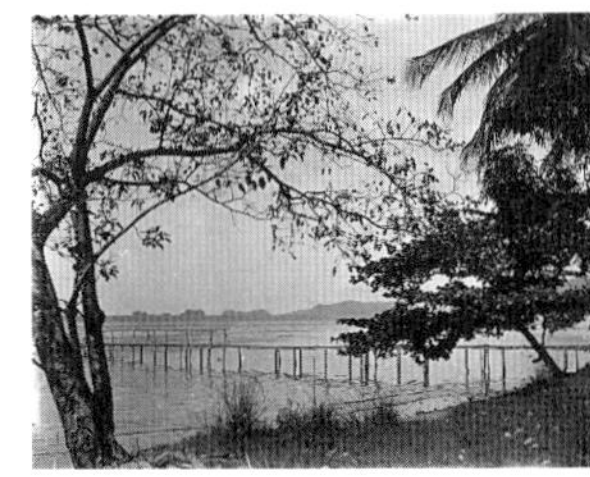

This is a view from a shaded grassy cove looking across to the northern end of the island. The photograph is taken from a small stretch of highway called the Foreshore. The five islands off the coast of Port of Spain that Trinidadians use for recreation are visible in the distance. The names of the islands are Diego, Gaspar Grande, Monos, Huevos, Chacachacare and Patos, reflecting Trinidad's Spanish, Amerindian and French heritage.

C926

68*

A Woman Selling Jack Fruit

Trinidad

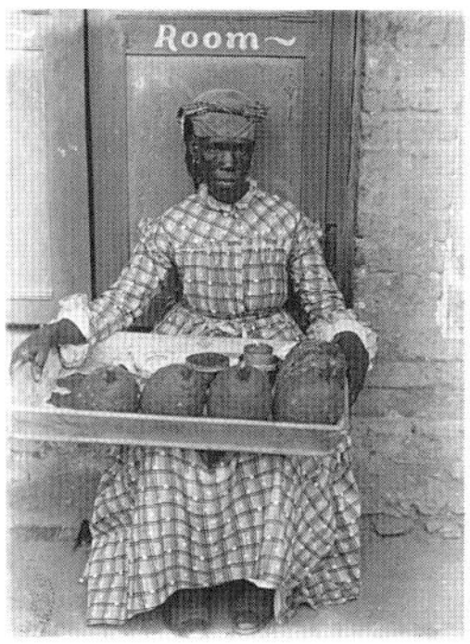

This woman sells breadfruit, *fruit de pain*, which Captain Bligh first attempted to bring to the Caribbean from Polynesia on his ship the Bounty when the infamous mutiny occurred in 1789. Four years later breadfruit was planted in the Caribbean to be used as a cheap nutritional staple for slaves. Johnston mistakes it for jackfruit, a meaty fruit of lemony-pineapple flavour, that looks similar and is also from the mulberry family. Since both were new to him, he could easily have been confused. The woman is captured against a doorway with the word 'room' written on it. This signage places the photograph in Port of Spain since that kind of advertising would be a city phenomenon.

C928

69*

Unripe Coconuts

Trinidad

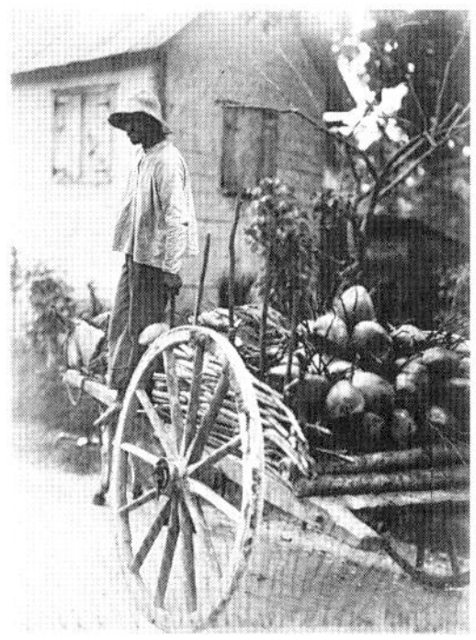

A young man with his dray laden with coconuts. Johnston calls the coconuts *'unripe'*, but they are in fact water coconuts sold for the tasty water and 'jelly' (soft fruit) inside. Coconut sellers then would have been drawn to urban areas, so he is probably in Port of Spain. This developing commercialism is a mark of modernity in the capital.

C877

70

A Negro House

Trinidad

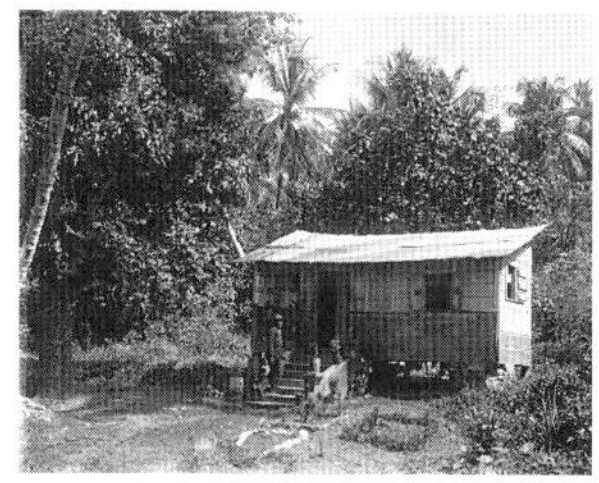

A large single glass plate negative, this landscape shows a small country house surrounded thickly by trees and other vegetation. With its mis-matched shutters and boarding, the house is a combination of wooden construction and concrete foundation, raised off the ground by bricks. Such structures are more typical of houses in the island's north and south east in places like Toco and Manzanilla. It is unlikely that Johnston travelled so far inland since his ship circuited the coast. More likely this house is just outside Port of Spain.

C931

Notes and References

1 For some of the problems inherent in this type of revisionism see William A.Green 'The Creolisation of History', in *Caribbean Freedom Economy and Society from Emancipation to the Present* 1993.

2 For discussions about this process of 'othering' with regard to Haiti and the Caribbean see: Michael Dash, *Haiti and the United States,* London, 1988, Chapter 1. For Western attitudes to the East see: Edward Said, *Orientalism* London, 1978 and with regard to Europe's attitude towards Africans see: Petrine Archer-Straw, *Negrophilia*, Ph.D. Thesis, Courtauld Institute, University of London, 1994.

3 For a discussion about how stereotypes are created and reinforced see: Homi Bhabi, 'The Other Question: The Stereotype and Colonial Discourse' *Screen* (London) Vol.24 p.6, November–December, 1983.

4 Sir Harry Johnston was knighted and had numerous awards including the C.B. (1890), K.C.B. (1896), and G.C.M.G. (1901). For the purposes of this essay he will be referred to as Harry Johnston.

5 The fact that many of the islands such as Barbados, Trinidad and Santa Domingo are so unevenly represented militates against exhibiting Johnston's photography geographically, island by island. Instead an integrated thematic presentation highlighting other significant themes in Johnston's work has been used such as landscapes, flora and fauna, architecture and genre scenes in addition to his interest in racial types.

6 For further discussion regarding the term 'New World' and its relevance to the Caribbean see the catalogue essay: Petrine Archer-Straw, 'Many Rivers Crossed' in 'New World Imagery: Contemporary Jamaican Art', National Touring Exhibitions, Hayward Gallery and Arts Council Collection, London, 1995.

7 By contrast labels accompanying the photographs in the exhibition have been presented without the same consideration for this type of post-modern critical interpretation. The emphasis in looking at these images has been on placing them within a historical context, providing sufficient knowledge about what and where they are so that in the Caribbean we can begin to flesh out limited visual knowledge of the past.

8 H.H. Johnston, *Negro in the New World* London, 1911, p.428.

9 H.H. Johnston, *The Black Man's Part in the War* London, 1917, p.106.

10 As Johnston had not been well prior to his trip taking Greaves as a companion and assistant was a necessity. Johnston tells us that much of the heavy duty work in carrying and setting up equipment was done by Greaves. What is less difficult to discern is whether Greaves had a hand in actually taking photographs.

11 See: H.H. Johnston, *The Story of My Life* London: Chatto and Windus, 1923, p.401 where Johnston discusses his invitation to the White House and Roosevelt's forthcoming trip to eastern Equatorial Africa. Preparation for Roosevelt's safari are subsequently reported in 'The Big Hunt', The Daily Gleaner, December 10, 1908, p.8, and March 22, 1908, p.8.

12 Although we have no record of the private conversations that took place between Roosevelt and Johnston, letters exchanged between the two men hint at this agenda. In particular, the national newspaper front page reprints a letter to Johnston in which Roosevelt writes, *'I do not think we shall intervene in Hayti. Of course, we ought to but this people of ours [Americans] simply does not understand how things are outside of our own boundaries. Of course, I do not not desire to act unless I can get the bulk of our people to understand the situation and to back up the action; and to do that I have got to get the facts vividly before them and clearly before them. In Panama, Cuba, Santa Domingo and Puerto Rico, it needed months or years of preparation before we could get our people to see things straight ... but the American people are simply not alive to the situation.'* 'Roosevelt Wanted to Interfere in Hayti: Important letter to Harry Johnston', *The Daily Gleaner*, Kingston Jamaica, 16 March 1909, p.1.

13 Under the presidency of Theodore Roosevelt and in keeping with expansionist policies of the era, America played an interventionist role in the Caribbean resulting in their governance of Cuba between 1906

and 1908 and their occupation of Haiti in 1915. It was reported in Jamaica's national newspaper that: *'In his annual message to congress in 1904, President Roosevelt said: Chronic wrongdoing or an impotence which results in a general loosening of the ties of civilised society may in America as elsewhere, ultimately require intervention by some civilised nation, and in the Western hemisphere and the adherence of the United States to the Munroe Doctrine may force the U.S. however reluctantly in flagrant case of such wrong doing or impotence to the exercise of international police power.'* See: *The Daily Gleaner* December 8, 1908, p.1.

14 For discussions of a similar nature see: Michael Dash, *Haiti and the United States,* London, 1988, p.12

15 Johnston visited Tuskegee College in Alabama, and Hampton College in Virginia and devoted several chapters of *Negro in the New World* to the education and conditions of negroes in the southern states of America.

16 A special project in Liberia in 1906 had aroused Johnston's curiosity regarding the African Diaspora and the creole community in what was considered an American protectorate.

17 The exhibition comprises seventy images selected from Harry Johnston's archive now stored at the Royal Geographical Society in London. The exhibition is not a true reflection of the complete archive. It shows the strongest and most poignant images from over a total of 1000 negatives of which about 300 are from the Caribbean. In this sense, this is an unbalanced presentation of Johnston's original vision. It places another bias on the prejudices that Johnston demonstrated in his photographic essay to show the condition of the *'negro in the new world'*. To some extent this distortion has been encouraged so as not to fall prey to Johnston's own biases where the Caribbean is viewed significantly in racial terms.

18 For an intimate portrait of Johnston's life and work see:Roy Kerridge 'In search of Sir Harry' *Spectator* 19 December, 1981.

19 Johnston is remembered for his discovery of the Okapi, *'a strange long-legged, velvet-skinned relative of the giraffe, which wanders the the shadowy depths of the Ituri Forest, home of the Pygmies'*. The species is now called the 'Okapia johnstoni'.

20 It was in this same manner that Johnston was appointed Commissioner of the British Protectorate of Nyasaland between 1893–1897.

21 By the 1880's, Johnston had embarked upon what would be his life's work, *A Comparative Study of the Bantu and Semi Bantu Languages,* eventually published in 1919.

22 See also: H.H. Johnston, *News and Reviews: From the Outlook of an Anthropologist* London, 1912.

23 Adolphe Duperley was the founder of Adolphe Duperley and Sons a family business run by three generations of Duperleys in Kingston, Jamaica, between 1840 and *c.*1930. Their studio work dominated portrait photography during these years. In 1844, Adolphe Duperley also published *Dageurrian Excursions in Jamaica* using the innovative daguerreotype process. See footnote 7.

24 Juan Baptista Valdez and his son John Valdez jnr. worked in both Jamaica and Cuba at different times. The father, Juan Baptista Valdez was renowned for his full length portrait of Jose Marti and his photography that earned a gold medal at the Paris World Fair of 1867. See below.

25 An exhibition containing photographs of this type was recently shown in Kingston Jamaica, see: Studio Art, *Photographs 1850–1940*, Kingston, Jamaica, 1997.

26 In A. Leader's *Through Jamaica with a Kodak* Bristol, 1907, Leader describes the vagaries and practicalities of kodak photography in Jamaica. He advises threepence to sixpence for the willing sitter and nickels to appease the crowds, claiming that *'The kodaking operation is a great source of merriment to the black crowd of onlookers, who joke the sitter or model and laugh uproarously as only the negro can.'* Despite the derogatory tone this indicates the very public nature of this type of photographic work. In terms of technique Leader also comments, *'... developing in a small dark room with the temperature above 90 degrees in the shade is terrible work; the perspiration drops off one during the process. Indeed, the difficulties of getting good results are great here, the ammonia of the developer evaporates almost before you can use it'.*

27 H.H. Johnston, *Negro in the New World*, London 1911.

28 A term and reading of slavery employed by Benitez-Rojo that aptly describes the dehumanising and purely exploitative nature of slavery. See Antonio Benitez-Rojo, *The Repeating Island*, Durham, 1992, p.4.

29 For a collection of such texts see Hilary Beckles and Verene Shepherd, *Caribbean Freedom Economy and Society from Emancipation to the Present* 1993.

30 See: Woodville Marshall 'We be wise to many more tings' in *Caribbean Freedom Economy and Society from Emancipation to the Present*, 1993, p.12–20.

31 See: Beverly Cary 'The Windward Maroons after the Peace Treaty', *Jamaica Journal*, Kingston, Jamaica, Vol.4, No.4, December 1970, p.19.

32 Johnston wrote about his trip to Maroon Town in his biography saying, *'This district did not seem to me entirely pacified even in 1909, and although I was as placatory as possible, the attitude of the people was somewhat surly and aggressive'*, see: H.H. Johnston, *The Story of My Life*, London 1923.

33 See Sidney Mintz *'Black Women, Economic Roles and Cultural Traditions'*, also David Trotman *'Women and Crime in Late 19th Century Trinidad'* and in Hilary Beckles and Verene Shepherd, *Caribbean Freedom Economy and Society from Emancipation to the Present*, 1993. With respect to this 'new breed' of femaleTrottman writes that their behaviour *'seemed directly opposed to the ideals of an elite influenced by Victorian ethics. Lower class behaviour seemed to emphasize noise, turmoil and lack of sobriety, decorum and respectability. The behaviour of lower class women in particular represented everything that was antithetical to ruling-class notions of respectability.'*

34 The *coup* took place on 2 December 1908. President Alexis was forcefully removed from power by General Antoine Simone, who assumed duties as President on 17 December 1908.

35 The poster announces that the inauguration will take place at the Race Course on the Champ de Mars, the parkland surrounding the President's palace.

36 Based on a conversation with Port Au Prince historian Georges Corvington, June 1997.

37 The sale of jelly coconuts would have been a recent phenomenon in Port of Spain to those more usually able to pick and drink their own.

38 Johnston also visited the Panama Canal as part of his tour of the region.

39 Because of ill-health, Johnston's trip to the Caribbean was his last extensive excursion. After that he retired to his country home in Poling, Sussex where he continued to write prolifically until his death of a stroke in 1927.

40 H.H. Johnston, *Negro in the New World*, London, 1911, p.482.

ROYAL GEOGRAPHICAL SOCIETY
(WITH THE INSTITUTE OF BRITISH GEOGRAPHERS)

The Royal Geographical Society (with The Institute of British Geographers) has, for over 160 years, been a national and international focus of geographical research, information and exploration. It is the largest and most vigorous geographical society in Europe with a membership of some 13,000.

The objectives of the Society are defined in its original Royal Charter, namely: 'the advancement of geographical science and the improvement and diffusion of geographical knowledge'. As part of these objectives the Society seeks to:

- Stimulate awareness, interest and enjoyment of geography and environmental matters in people of all ages and from all backgrounds. Geography today encompasses the most urgent global issues and many social and physical environmental challenges of the 1990s.
- Act as an authoritative voice representing and promoting geography and geographers in Britain and overseas.
- Act as a focus for geographical research and initiating, supporting and, where possible, funding geographical research, including field projects overseas.
- Promote and enhance the value of geography in education, with particular reference to higher education.
- Provide a national geographical information resource and a database of geographical expertise.
- Give training and advice to those organising expeditions.

The Society serves the geographical interests of a wide range of people, including those in geographical-related professions; academics, researchers and teachers; sixth-form, undergraduate and postgraduate students; those wishing to keep in touch with geography; and those with a wider interest in the human and physical environment, travel and exploration.